AMERICAN LOG HOMES

AMERICAN LOG HOMES

by Arthur Thiede and Cindy Teipner

 Rodale Press, Emmaus, Pa.

Printed in Italy by New Interlitho S.P.A.

Senior editor: Ray Wolf
Copy editor: Rebecca Jones
Book design by Karen A. Schell
Illustrations by Frank Rohrbach
Photography by Arthur Thiede and Cindy Teipner
(aerial photo of Double Fork Ranch by Robert Bichsel; photo of St. John's Hospital by Parthenia Stinnett courtesy of Jackson Historical Society; photos of Culloden Farm courtesy of the owners)

Library of Congress Cataloging in Publication Data
Thiede, Arthur.
　　American log homes.

　　Bibliography: p.
　　Includes index.
　　1. Log cabins—United States.　　I. Teipner, Cindy.
II. Title
NA8470.T48　　1986　　728.3'7'0973　　85-25633
ISBN　0-87857-607-X　hardcover
2　4　6　8　10　9　7　5　3　1　hardcover

If you have built castles in the air, your work need not be lost; there is where they should be. Now put foundations under them.
—Henry David Thoreau

CONTENTS

PREFACE

When we set out to write a book documenting log homes in America, we felt certain it had not been done before. Three years and 40,000 miles later, we began to understand why.

It was no coincidence that we started hunting for log houses in our hometown of Ketchum, Idaho. We have long been intrigued by the diversity and originality of local log homes. Our initial survey revealed small, stereotypical log cabins as well as new, exciting log designs. We saw how architects, builders, and other craftsmen have transformed the spartan log home into something more befitting of the times. Log building has come of age.

There are enough log structures in our region to form the basis for a book, but we decided a national scope would more accurately represent American log building. By traveling throughout the country, we hoped to record many building styles and glean valuable insight into historical log building and design.

And so we set out in search of the American Log Home.

We rebuilt our 12-year-old Dodge van and filled it to the luggage rack with food, clothes, camera gear, road maps, and great expectations. Over the next three years, we would spend weeks and months at a stretch tracking and backtracking America's maze of roadways in search of unique log homes.

Word of mouth and directions scribbled on matchbooks and cafe napkins were often our only road maps. After talking with log-home owners, architects, and builders—and with bystanders ranging from backwoods hermits to grocery store clerks—we realized that everyone harbors his or her own image of the quintessential log home. All too often, we chased grand recollections down miles of rough road only to find a cockeyed cabin in the woods.

But for every futile search ending in a flat tire or a "trespassers will be shot" sign, there was another that had us knocking on doors and loading our cameras. In the end, we photographed hundreds of buildings from Connecticut to California, from Ketchum to Kentucky.

As we rolled back into Ketchum from the last of many trips, we reflected on the breakdowns, black flies, missed shots, and missed turns. Our wallets were worn as thin as our tires, and we were exhausted—but we were still talking to each other. And we were enriched by our discovery of the homes you will find presented in the following pages.

ACKNOWLEDGMENTS

During the course of our travels throughout America to photograph homes for *American Log Homes,* we met hundreds of people who graciously helped us in many ways. Though we kept careful diaries and can account for most of you, it would be impossible not to pass up someone if we tried to list all your names. To preclude that possibility, we would like this to serve as a blanket acknowledgment to all those concerned. Thank you very much.

INTRODUCTION

The log house embodies an ingenious building technique. Hewn from the forest with only an axe, logs were used by early settlers to create the houses that became the dominant form of shelter on the American frontier. As such, these houses—the fabled pioneer log cabins—assumed a special place in our national consciousness. They came to represent the resourcefulness and rugged determination of the pioneer. Their secure and cozy image is fixed in American folklore, on maple syrup tins, and, certainly, in the hearts of many who grew up with Lincoln Logs.

With the advent of sawmills, log building ceased to be a practical and efficient way to build. As the frontier became civilized, people no longer wanted these homes of the wilderness. Today, however, things have come full circle. The log house is regaining its rightful place as a popular form of American home building.

Over the last few decades, interest in home designs of the past has undergone a resurgence. There has been a revival of our architectural heritage as evidenced by the renewed popularity of adobe homes, Victorian homes, and—most important for the subject of this book—log homes.

Central to the renewed interest in log construction has been a basic change in the image of log homes. In the past,

the mention of a log home usually brought to mind a small cabin: a rustic shelter in the wilderness. Slightly dark, slightly musty, a place you might visit—but not a place where you would want to live.

Today, all that has changed. Modern log construction has ample flexibility to meet contemporary demands for comfort, convenience, and aesthetic pleasure. While some people believe the parameters of log design are too restrictive, this book demonstrates otherwise, and it pays tribute to those who have lent their imagination and verve to the evolution of log building. The sheer variety and beauty of the homes shown in this book demonstrate conclusively that logs are a practical, enduring, and inherently beautiful building material. Anyone thinking of building a home today should certainly consider the possibility of using logs.

The revival of log construction has prompted the growth of a billion-dollar industry. Thousands of log homes are erected annually throughout the United States. The dream of handcrafting a home still drives dedicated men and women into the woods with axes and chainsaws. But the great majority of the houses being built from logs today are anything but primitive. Most log-house owners hire architects and professional builders. Or they purchase precut, peeled, and notched logs from one of the many log-building companies

scattered throughout the United States and Canada.

The explosive growth of the log-construction industry has surprised many building professionals. What was originally perceived as a small, second home or vacation home market has expanded into a market for primary residences as well. Having explored the extent and direction of this log-building revival, we offer this book as a tribute to the enduring legacy of log homes in American architecture.

In selecting photographs for the book, our intent was not to emphasize the cost or size of the homes shown, but to illustrate the homes' architectural merits. Photographs illuminating many different building styles, old and new, are included to illustrate design evolution from both chronological and geographic perspectives.

Today's log houses often defy traditional design boundaries by incorporating materials other than logs. For example, the marriage of logs with such diverse elements as stucco, tile, and copper permits more architectural flexibility. Combining traditional and modern elements, modern dualistic designs have eased the way for the return of log homes to the mainstream of American shelter. So look to these homes for inspiration. Borrow from them appropriate ideas and concepts, and create your own American Log Home.

HISTORICAL PERSPECTIVES

The exact origin of log building is lost in prehistory, but archaeologists have suggested that the form arose with the peoples of northern Europe during the Bronze Age. Armed with crude but effective tools, inhabitants of the dense north woods confronted and utilized vast stretches of virgin forest. They cleared trees for crop planting and used the tall, straight timbers to build sturdy, practical shelters.

The Scandinavians and peoples of northern Russia were probably the first to establish a log-building tradition. With light, easily shaped softwood in abundant supply, they eventually refined log construction and design into highly developed forms. Particularly impressive are some of the elaborate buildings fashioned by the Russians as early as the 16th century. Among the finest examples are churches towering more than 150 log courses high. Because of careful design and excellent craftsmanship, these structures have endured the elements for hundreds of years. They stand today as testimony to the longevity of logs as a building material.

Approximately two decades after the arrival of the Pilgrims at Plymouth, Swedish and Finnish immigrants brought European log building to America. Contrary to popular belief, the Pilgrims knew nothing of log-cabin living. Instead, they sought traditional housing and laboriously set out reducing vast forests to hewn lumber and whipsawn boards. Scandinavians settled the area we now call Delaware in 1638. They brought both the knowledge and skills needed to manipulate whole logs into secure and sturdy abodes. Using only axes, they could raise a suitable cabin in a single day: a decisive advantage in the hostile environs of an unsettled land.

Over the next 75 years, Swedes and Finns did the majority of log building on the eastern seaboard. Then, early in the 18th century, German immigrants settling in Pennsylvania employed their knowledge of wood to further propagate the log cabin throughout the American frontier.

Thousands of immigrants followed, searching for adventure, independence, and prosperity in the New World. The abundance of trees made the log home a logical choice. Newcomers who had little or no log-building heritage, like the Scotch and Irish, were quick to adopt the building techniques honed by Scandinavian and German craftsmen.

As the log cabin spread westward with the impatient pursuits of a diverse population, ethnic groups imbued cabin design with elements reflecting their particular cultures. Design also responded more and more to individual needs. Different methods of building evolved through adaptation of existing forms. The frontier log cabin thus came to represent an amalgam of architectural styles: truly American in every sense of the word.

It is generally acknowledged that the Swedes and Germans had the greatest effect on log building in the New World.

But the French contributed an important style variation. Instead of traveling overland through the developing colonies on the Atlantic Coast, the French paddled their pirogues across the lakes and rivers of eastern Canada. They established their presence independently of other colonists, settling along the Mississippi River. Rather than erecting their log walls by laying logs horizontally on top of each other, French Canadians stood logs vertically, rooting them in the earth or placing them on rock sills. The interstices between the vertical logs were filled with *bouzillage*, a binding mixture of clay or mud combined with straw, twigs, or animal hair.

Vertical log construction was used primarily for stockade building. Another French innovation proved very useful in home construction. Called *pieces-sur-pieces*, or piece-on-piece, the method was especially suited for building with small logs. Previously, cabin design had been restricted by the girth and length of the wall logs. A cabin usually consisted of a single rectangular room called a pen or den. The length of the room was equal to the length of the logs. Larger homes were built by joining two or more of these simple cabins to each other.

French settlers, however, discovered that by attaching the ends of horizontal logs to a series of vertical posts, walls could be extended to any length. The buildings erected with this system could be quite large, but the logs themselves could be short and light, requiring fewer hands for the construction work—an important point when the nearest neighbors were often many miles away.

Log structures of the frontier period were notched and detailed in many ways, while the logs themselves were either left round or hewn flat on one or more sides. The introduction of hewn-log construction, with its diversity of corner notching, is hard to trace. We know the Pennsylvania Germans applied this technique along with dovetail or swallowtail notching, but the influence of the English cannot be overlooked. With their strong shipbuilding background and heritage of half-timber architecture, it would have been a logical approach for them.

Building a hewn-log house requires considerably more time and effort than a round-log house. As a result, the pioneer builder would reserve this method for his most cherished projects. According to Charles McRaven, author of *Building the Hewn Log House*, the settler's first shelter and outbuildings might consist of round logs, but the permanent home deserved additional craftsmanship. From a practical standpoint, the lifespan of a hewn structure is much longer since the outer bark and decay-prone sap wood are removed from the logs. In addition, flat interior walls evoke a certain dignity of style. To the pioneer woman, smooth walls were reminiscent of the culture and comforts left behind. They helped turn rugged wilderness cabins into comfortable homes.

Nevertheless, hewn-log building gained favor only in settlements east of the Mississippi. The dominant frontier housing in the fast push westward consisted of log cabins built quickly and, in most cases, crudely. The frenzied rush for land, gold, and glory led homesteaders to throw together round-log cabins by the thousands. Later, when these settlers considered building more refined shelters, milled lumber had arrived on the building scene, so second-generation homes were usually built not of hewn logs but of lumber processed in a mill. Wilderness yielded to technology. Anything packaged, polished, or refined was gladly embraced. It seemed the American log-building era had ended.

But as log cabins grew scarce, the myth of these wilderness homes became entrenched in American folklore. Log building was no longer necessary, but nostalgic notions of bygone days kept it alive. And around the turn of the 20th century, log building enjoyed a glorified resurgence. Under the leadership of William A. Durrant, president of the Adirondack Railroad and developer par excellence, the Great Camps of the Adirondacks were established for the wealthy aristocracy of New York City. The buildings erected at these woodland camps hardly resembled shelter built of necessity. Though constructed with logs, the buildings' size and amenities far exceeded anything on the frontier. These structures heralded a new approach to log building. For the first time in American history, log construction and design was directed by professional architects. Undoubtedly, the camps and the log structures inspired by them led a new generation of Americans to rethink old biases toward houses built of logs.

Architects throughout the country designed buildings similar to those at the Adirondack camps. Numerous private hideaways, exclusive hunting retreats, and National Park lodges all contributed to romantic—though often distorted—notions of "log-cabin living." Perhaps most famous of all is Yellowstone National Park's Old Faithful Inn. Built in 1904, this log marvel boasts an eight-story lobby rising 185 feet. There are 140 rooms, three sets of balconies, a widow's walk, and even a crow's nest. Add to this the fact that construction began and continued through one of the coldest winters in Wyoming's history, and you have one remarkable building achievement!

Usually, the builders and owners of the new log structures never intended them to serve as permanent residences. They considered them vacation cabins or lodges at summer resorts. Though pretentious, these "rustic" retreats of

the wealthy sparked enthusiasm for less grandiose log construction, and the log home's popularity has slowly increased ever since.

Perhaps surprisingly, another factor contributing to log building's new nationwide appeal was the Great Depression. As the country's economy struggled back to its feet in the 1930s, the federal government established the Works Progress Administration (WPA) and the Civilian Conservation Corps (CCC) in an effort to aid thousands of unemployed citizens. Working through the U.S. Forest Service and the National Park Service, the men and women in these programs built thousands of log structures throughout our national forests and parks. They built lookout towers, ranger stations, lodges, and bridges. Erected primarily for utility, many of these buildings were fine examples of the log builders' craft. They were among the first real log structures many people had ever seen. Better than pictures from a history text, more real than Lincoln Logs, these buildings played an important role in the evolution of American log building.

Born of necessity on the frontier and then recast by the dreams and romantic notions of ensuing generations, log building represents important elements of the American spirit. This legacy, though ever-changing, surely will continue for many years to come.

CHIEF JOSEPH RANCH

LOCATION Darby, Montana • ARCHITECT Bates and Gamble • BUILDERS Various

Open range stretches from the river-rock archways of the Chief Joseph Ranch. It is a rugged setting for this mighty log home.

William Ford, thought to have been influenced by Yellowstone's Old Faithful Inn, had this ranch house built in 1914 at a cost of $50,000. That year, 24 carpenters began construction

This imaginative mix of curving roof lines, vertical logs, and uniquely patterned windows defies notions that log buildings were simple structures built only of necessity.

with logs cut from the nearby Tincup Creek area. The ridge log, some 120 feet long, attests to the hefty structural and architectural achievement of the builders.

The ranch house, with its diverse collection of arches, dormers, hips, and sweeping gables, represents the architects' first attempt at log home design. A massive structure, the home is graced with unexpected elegance.

Ford and his family spent summers here, arriving by train at the small neighboring town of Darby, Montana. The train no longer stops in Darby, but little else has changed. The Chief Joseph Ranch stands as a fitting monument to its

In an era before attached garages and sliding glass doors, architects placed great emphasis on the entry to the house. Here, massive double arches leave no doubt as to where a visitor knocks.

builders and architects, as well as to its namesake: Chief Joseph of the Nez Percé tribe, who led his people through this valley in their monumental struggle to reach Canada on the Trail of Tears.

JACKSON LOG BUILDINGS

LOCATION Jackson, Wyoming • ARCHITECTS Various • BUILDERS Various

Jackson, Wyoming, has a heritage of log building that reaches back to its founding in 1897. With vast amounts of lodgepole pine nearby, most early buildings were constructed of logs. Because lodgepole pines tend to grow in dense stands, they are usually very straight, are uniform in size, and possess few limbs. These qualities make the species ideal for log building.

The Gill home, pictured here, is just one of many dating back to the town's early days. Owned by Helen Gill, whose husband opened Jackson's first saloon after the repeal of prohibition, the house has been expanded extensively. What started as a simple one-story log cabin has grown much larger over the years.

The other buildings pictured are St. John's Hospital and St. John's Episcopal Church. These also are fine examples of early Jackson log architecture.

Lodgepole pine seems more susceptible to disease than most tree species and, as a result, offers uniquely shaped limbs. Here they make intriguing braces for a covered picnic area. This backyard fun spot was built several years after the construction of the original house.

During World War II, Helen Gill worked as a nurse at St. John's. For a time, the hospital served its purpose well. However, long ago the sturdy, old building was cut into pieces and moved away, with each section going to a different place.

This early Jackson log building, a church, attests to the consistency and straightness of logs once available in the nearby forests. It is especially interesting because of the log dormers. These are difficult to build and, therefore, uncommon in many log structures.

LINCOLN'S BOYHOOD HOME

LOCATION Spencer County, Indiana • ARCHITECT Unknown • BUILDER Rebuilt by the National Park Service

Many Americans' first exposure to log building came from reading about Abe Lincoln in grade school history books. Though five previous U.S. presidents had been born in log cabins, the association between log cabins and the stuff presidents are made of is inevitably associated with Lincoln. So politically endearing was Lincoln's log-cabin image that, in 1950, presidential hopeful Senator Robert Kerr proclaimed proudly that he, too, was born in a log cabin.

But Lincoln gave us more than just a folksy staple of U.S. politics: His name was to become synonymous with one of the most beloved of all toys in America's history, Lincoln Logs.

Generations of boys and girls grew up with these sets of little logs that greatly influenced the course of log building. During the three decades following World War II, when most of America plunged into architectural chaos, those millions of Lincoln Log sets in toy chests around the country kept alive the romance of a life-style more attractive than the one families saw unfolding in Quonset huts, mobile homes, and tract-built ranch houses.

A pioneer home, this cabin had only one room, shared by the entire family. They slept in one half, cooked and ate in the other.

The work shed was a crucially important outbuilding. Here the homesteader made everything from horseshoes to farm implements.

Favored by many early log builders, poplar trees were used extensively in frontier shelters. Apart from being very decay-resistant, they actually strengthened with age. The logs in this cabin are about 150 years old yet are still in fine shape.

EMPIRE MANSION

LOCATION Denver, Colorado • ARCHITECT Unknown • BUILDER Unknown

As the American frontier pushed westward, Denver became a thriving metropolis where mining, ranching, and railroading infused huge amounts of money into the economy. Because Denver was virtually isolated from other major centers of commerce and industry, communications became vital to its growth.

In 1879, Frederick O. Vaille—who had come to Colorado the year before—established a telephone exchange that would eventually become the Colorado Telephone Company. Associated with Alexander Graham Bell, Vaille's company played an instrumental role in Denver's development.

The house shown here was built in 1911 as a summer home for Vaille. It is located in what is now called the Englewood district of Denver. Though the suburban environment seems incongruous with the house today, the cattle guards crossing the driveway reflect more bucolic times.

Originally the house was a series of small rooms located to either side of a central breezeway. This style was known by the eastern colloquialism of "dog-trot design" (presumably the family dogs were free to trot through the open breezeways of early dog-trot homes). The breezeway at Vaille's home was eventually enclosed to become a formal entry.

Numerous remodelings over the years make it difficult to determine which parts of the present structure form the original house and which parts were added later. We do know, however, that in 1939 a major renovation added much formality to the design. The upper-story logs were covered with scalloped boards, and the elaborately detailed gothic entry was also added. Through the addition of many other details, the building acquired a look very unlike its original rustic appearance.

ABOVE: The original walls of this magnificent mansion were log all the way to the roof. Later, boarding over the upper story logs gave a more dignified appearance to the building.

LEFT: Intricate handiwork is found on the windows where fleur-de-lis patterns crown the trim. The logs are not scribe-fitted, yet they match so closely that a minimum of chinking was needed.

The den is one of the few rooms where logs are visible indoors. Here they have been sanded smooth and finished to a rich lustre while decorative cord is affixed along the chink lines. Still, one might hardly notice the logs amid the glow of this embellished fireplace and ornate ceiling.

The opulent surroundings of the home are carried through to the dining room, where the textured ceiling and richly paneled walls cry out once again that this isn't just any log home. Hand-painted china and needlepoint chairs are the owners' own work.

AMK RANCH

LOCATION Jackson Lake, Grand Teton National Park, Wyoming • ARCHITECTS Unknown •
BUILDERS Johnson House: Charlie Fox; Berol House: Slim Lawrence

The AMK Ranch has served many owners in its colorful history. The structures that remain today represent some unique log-building styles.

Homesteaded in 1890, the ranch passed through a succession of owners before Lou Johnson and his wife bought it in 1927. Johnson hired Charlie Fox, the first contractor in the region, to build the two-story home pictured here. The house was unusual in its day because logs were still stacked by hand, and two stories were appreciably more difficult to build than one. Local residents say that Mrs. Johnson was so frightened by bears that she would settle for nothing less than a second-floor bedroom.

After three years, the finished building stood 25 log courses high and was among the area's tallest. Its style drew from the design of New England farm houses: New England farmers would build a large barn only a few feet from the main house, connected by a covered breezeway.

Another special feature is the screened front porch. Few are seen today, but at that time they were quite popular. In hot summer months, they gave welcome respite from swarms of flies and mosquitoes. Architecturally, the porch adds a handsome dimension to the building.

When Johnson died in 1934, A. C. Berol purchased the ranch. He would not be outdone by the architectural achievements of former owners—nor would he copy them.

Berol had his own ideas about log-home design, which are embodied in the new ranch house Slim Lawrence erected for him. Only five years separate the building dates of the Johnson and Berol houses, but they are light years apart in design. Whereas Johnson's boxy home has a folksy charm, Berol's sprawling structure makes a more modern statement. With its sharp angles, the design is surprisingly contemporary.

LEFT: *The second story provided Mrs. Johnson with a haven safe from bears. It also enabled an inspired craftsman to design and build this distinctive stairway leading to the bedroom.*

Curly wood sections used for posts and braces on the front porch lend much to the Johnson home's appeal. It takes a discerning eye to find these sculptures in the forest, but the reward is well worth the effort.

ABOVE: In 1935 Slim Lawrence set a crew to building Berol's house. The trees were cut, then skidded from the woods by horse and laid up for winter to season. In testimony to the builders' skill, the notches and joints are as tight today as when first cut.

RIGHT: Looking at the framework for the entry roof, you can appreciate just how solidly this structure has been built. The log posts supporting the tripled log plates are almost three feet in diameter.

ABOVE: Facing the lake, this hexagonal log bay served as a formal dining room where up to 40 guests could be seated. The foundation beneath the bay was poured in forms to resemble clapboard siding.

RIGHT: Above the hexagonal bay, the roof framing consists of hip and common rafters radiating from two king posts. Purlins between the rafters support the roof decking and add to the design.

SEKON LODGE

LOCATION Adirondack Mountains, New York • ARCHITECT Unknown • BUILDER Unknown

Comprising some two million acres in upper New York State, the Adirondack Park is a natural environment of unparalleled beauty. The area is also home to the Great Camps that were established by the wealthy aristocracy of New York City around the turn of the century.

These camps played an important role in the development of the park and catalyzed a revival of log building throughout the country. Few people, however, could afford to build on so massive a scale. To understand the size and design of these camps one must delve into their era.

Sekon Lodge, built in 1898 and renovated following a fire in 1902, is typical of the approximately 30 Great Camps established around this time. Situated on Upper Saranac Lake, the camp consisted of about 15 buildings, including guest quarters, servant quarters, a main lodge, dining halls, boat houses, and workshops.

Isaac Seligman, a prosperous banker from New York, owned Sekon. He would travel up from New York City, leaving at 7:00 A.M. and arriving at the Adirondacks rail terminus in early evening. He would then board a lake steamer, arriving at his camp in time for a late dinner. Throughout the summer, he would stay at his retreat for a week or two at a time.

Though wilderness retreats, the Great Camps hardly forced their inhabitants to rough it. The aristocracy figured the

The epitome of Adirondack design and architecture, this living room and fireplace depict the contrast between rustic birch-bark detailing and the rich look of doors and wall paneling.

logs in the walls and the bearskin rugs on the floors provided as much of a rustic experience as they needed.

While social and economic status no doubt influenced the size of these camps, a more practical consideration also played a role. Nearby towns were practically nonexistent and bringing in supplies was difficult, so self-sufficiency was required.

As the novelty of the camps began to wear thin, the expense of maintaining them skyrocketed. An episode of American log building ended, leaving ample evidence of its glory.

LEFT: Adding to the building's rusticity are logs with their bark left intact. This feature, along with covered breezeways and diamond grilled windows, were common in "Great Camp" architecture.

RIGHT: While not originally a dining room, this little alcove serves its present owners as an informal eating area. Once again, the elaborate birch bark detailing dominates the interior design.

KOOTENAI LODGE

LOCATION Big Fork, Montana • ARCHITECT Kirtland Cutter • BUILDER Unknown

Rapid industrialization during the 19th and early 20th centuries created personal fortunes that were truly awesome. Wealth was accumulated at a staggering pace—a pace unretarded by nuisances like corporate and personal income taxes. With enormous sums of money at their disposal, industrial magnates would purchase thousands of acres for personal wilderness retreats. Such was the origin of Kootenai Lodge, modeled after the Adirondack Great Camps.

Designed by Kirtland Cutter, the Kootenai estate consisted of 14 log and stone buildings. It was owned by Cornelius "Con" Kelley, president of the Anaconda Copper Mining Company. The overall design of Kootenai is related to the Great Camps, but Cutter developed a style distinctively his own.

Cutter's choice of construction materials is a trademark of his style. While most of the wall logs are tamarack, all the posts in the buildings are western red cedar. The cedar logs were carefully hand carried from the forest to the house site so as to retain their delicate bark. The contrast formed by the peeled smoothness of the walls and the rough texture of the posts is a Cutter trademark.

The estate contains many well-designed buildings, but Cutter focused his talents on the lodge. The main building is flanked by guest quarters, forming a courtyard. And with the basketball-court–size great room indoors, "Con" Kelley could entertain in grand style regardless of the weather.

Why not? Though remote, the lodge was never a lonely retreat. Such notable personalities as John D. Rockefeller, Charles Lindbergh, and Will Rogers stayed at the lodge, adding their charisma to its already irresistible charm.

As happened to countless estates conceived during the Gilded Age, Kootenai's heyday was brief. By the 1940s, the lodge had fallen into disuse and disrepair. Boarded up and forgotten for the next three decades, Kootenai has recently been resurrected as a time-share resort. The new owners are pumping in large amounts of money and energy to reclaim the splendor and charm that was once Kootenai Lodge.

Here, in the courtyard, are the guest quarters where "Con" Kelley put up his renowned visitors. It was in this corner of the patio that Charles Russell entertained himself by sketching in the concrete.

LEFT: *Several of the guest cabins have these arched or "bell" roofs. These were framed using dimensioned lumber and are a trademark of the architect, Kirtland Cutter.*

RIGHT: *Most guest cabins on the property have been warmly remodeled and are ready for visitors. Here, the fireplace evidences the exemplary stone work common throughout the estate.*

BELOW: *About the size of a basketball court, the "great" room of the main lodge was the place for social gatherings. Though it was abandoned for many generations, many of the original furnishings survived intact.*

THE TIMBERS

LOCATION Long Lake, Michigan • ARCHITECT Arthur Huen • BUILDERS Morrison Kistler and Frank Grapes

The main house of the J. Ogden Armour estate in central Michigan represents the flamboyance and wealth of the same era that saw the creation of Sekon and Kootenai Lodges.

Responding to his wife's wishes more than his own, Armour financed the creation of the estate at a time when his meat-packing firm was reeling from the cancellation of huge government contracts at the end of World War I. Despite losses of up to a million dollars a day, Armour was hardly in financial straits. With a fortune that can only be imagined, he was able to employ a large portion of Long Lake Township's population to build his estate.

Taking almost a decade to complete, the estate was wholly self-sufficient, with a power plant, farm, orchards, main buildings, servant quarters, water supply, boat houses, greenhouses, and vineyards. All told, the estate boasted some 30 bedrooms, 13 baths, and a living room that could accommodate 125 people. Not bad for a summer residence.

The main building appears to be constructed of full-round logs, but it was actually framed with dimensioned lumber. Half-round logs were applied to the walls as siding. Heightening the deception are full-round log corners that were skillfully added to the walls. This practice of veneering logs to a building was common during the period. Apparently the wealthy, who built most of these summer camps, were not prepared to completely abandon their luxurious lifestyles

even while "roughing it" for the summer: They wanted a rustic appearance, but only within strict limits.

Building materials such as rock and logs serve to complement each other as natural elements of construction. Their use is evident throughout the estate.

This colorful, storybook home was built for Ogden's faithful secretary and willed to her upon his death. Situated about a quarter-mile from the main house, it was beautifully landscaped and had its own outbuildings, including a boat house.

ABOVE: *Instead of using mortar as chinking, the builders of The Timbers scribed boards to fit between the logs. Painted white, the boards fool even the most discerning eye.*

RIGHT: *The overall design of the house contains many bays. In each, the logs are butted to corner posts instead of overlapping. This makes for cleaner, less cluttered additions.*

Few bay windows are as attractive as these. The shutters are not only built using raised panels, but all feature differently designed cutouts depicting a variety of insects, mammals, and birds.

The distinctive rock corner columns are a mark of the creative flair that adds an unusual but interesting dimension to The Timbers. Note, too, the use of vertical logs in the gable end.

While this small structure may look like a guest cottage, it is really a child's playhouse. Nevertheless, its construction, like everything else at The Timbers, is first class.

The unusual roof of this entry has vertical logs in the gable end. Rounded eaves give the effect of a thatched roof, distinguishing the architecture here from the main house.

TRAIL TOWN

LOCATION Cody, Wyoming • ARCHITECTS Various • BUILDERS Various

This museum in Cody, Wyoming, represents the lifetime commitment by its owner, Bob Edgar, to save and display structures and memorabilia of the Old West. This is not a Disneyland frontier town—the buildings here are authentic.

They were painstakingly disassembled, moved, and then reassembled here at the museum. What you see is what Edgar saw over the years as he traveled throughout western Wyoming to salvage these treasures of the past.

Architecturally, they are important because they show what types of buildings were constructed on the frontier. The diversity of building styles is surprising, ranging from the crude cabin the government built for one of General Custer's scouts to a more refined downtown building with its characteristic false front. They are all here, filled with artifacts Edgar accumulated over the years.

Recalling times when many buildings were nothing but basic "shelter from the storm," these austere structures offer an historical perspective on American log building.

Here is a building style found typically in the western frontier town. The "false front" was often added to community structures to present a more dignified and imposing facade.

Historically, western log buildings were crude compared to the finely hewn buildings east of the Mississippi. This example was built by our government for General Custer's Indian scout, Curly.

TIE-HACK BUILDINGS

LOCATION Dubois, Wyoming • ARCHITECT Unknown • BUILDER Unknown

The history of American log building is a chronicle of great variety. The story of Abraham Lincoln's log home is well known, and millions of tourists have seen the Yellowstone Inn. But the small town of DuBois, Wyoming, can lay claim to an important chapter in the history of log building, too.

The story focuses not on a building or architect, but on the Wyoming tie hack.

As the railroads spread at the turn of the century, an insatiable demand for wooden railroad ties was born. Tie

companies quickly discovered that the dense lodgepole forests in the Wind River Range of western Wyoming could help meet this demand. Consequently, company towns were carved from the forest so tie-making operations could begin. Skilled axemen erected the buildings. These were not crude, hastily built shelters, but buildings tight and strong enough to withstand fierce Wyoming storms. Included were cabins, workshops, schoolhouses, laundries, cook houses, and dining halls. Only after their town was completed could the tough woodsmen go into the forest to cut ties.

The difference between a tie hack and a lumberjack is often confused. Though they both felled trees for a living, the tie hack's main work started after the tree was down, whereas the lumberjack's task was essentially finished. The tie hack would hew two flat surfaces on opposite sides of the log, to create a railroad tie. This demanded impressive skill. The railroad would not accept ties thicker than 7¾ inches nor thinner than 7 inches, so a careful eye and accurate swing were needed to produce the 8-foot-long ties.

The best tie hacks were so adept at their work that they could produce 50 ties a day. And each day's work included cutting a road to the chosen stand of trees and stacking all the ties after they were hewn! So efficient were the hacks' techniques that their successors continued hand-hewing ties into the 1940s, even though most companies had portable engine-driven saws at their disposal. One company alone, operating near DuBois, cut more than 10 million ties from 1900 to 1940, and nearly all were hand-hewn.

In the lobby of this Dubois log structure, now a motel, a balcony wraps around the entire room. Downstairs, hand-painted furnishings provide a cozy retreat before a polished stone fireplace.

SNAKE RIVER RANCH

LOCATION Jackson Hole, Wyoming • ARCHITECT Paul Coborn • BUILDER Marley Jones

Built in 1931, this log ranch house has two features that distinguish its architectural lineage. Both the log chimney and the two-story construction are rooted in the architecture of the eastern United States. Yet this structure was erected far to the west—it was, in fact, one of the first two-story log houses ever built in the Jackson Hole area of Wyoming.

The log chimney is like those found in the oldest eastern log cabins. Logs lined with clay were used instead of stones.

Popular in many older log homes, the balcony served as access to upper-story rooms and as an interesting piece of interior design in itself. Note the detailing in the rail.

The projecting roof eaves protected the clay from rain. Usually built in areas that lacked native stone, this style of chimney is uncommon to Jackson Hole. Its selection was no doubt influenced by the building's architect, a native of Connecticut.

Vast forests of lodgepole pine surround Jackson Hole. Thus, log building has always been a popular form of construction here. Hundreds of log structures attest to the earliest days of Jackson Hole's history. This strong heritage of log building has provided much of the impetus for its revival in Jackson Hole today.

The wall opposite the balcony includes a tall expanse of windows offering an eyeful of the distant Teton Range. The size of the windows adds an elegant touch and is very unusual in such an old home.

ADAPTIVE RESTORATIONS

The American landscape is graced with a diversity of architecture unequaled in the world. Contributing to this legacy, log buildings have been erected in a wide variety of styles, shapes, and sizes. Creating barns, churches, schoolhouses, courthouses, and just plain houses, early American log builders employed an amazing array of techniques. They produced structures that varied from the finely crafted hewn-log houses of the Pennsylvania Dutch to the prairie homesteaders' "dugouts" built of round logs with the bark intact.

Fortunately, many state and local historical groups have restored specimens of these old structures so we can study them. Perhaps even more fortunately, many other old log buildings still survive, available for restoration. Doing such restoration work—adapting an old log building for contemporary living—is the subject of this chapter.

Restoration begins with finding an abandoned log building, preferably one that is in good repair. Usually the structure is then dismantled and moved to another location, where the logs are used in combination with new materials to create a new building. The resulting structure thus incorporates elements of the original building supplemented by the benefits of modern technology—it is not a simple restoration; it is an *adaptive* restoration, one that is adapted to our contemporary needs and desires.

Why would someone go through all the trouble of finding and dismantling a log cabin just to get some old logs with which to build a new house? Wouldn't it be easier just to cut new logs? Understanding the logic behind the process requires examining some completed adaptive restorations from both a structural and philosophical perspective.

First, the majority of these projects involved the restoration of hewn-log buildings: structures with logs skillfully hewn flat on two sides then joined at the corners by a variety of notching techniques. Although a few craftsmen today can hew logs for a house, they are a vanishing breed. The skill, dedication, patience, and determination necessary for such an undertaking are qualities that, for the most part, disappeared with the frontier.

Second, finding timbers like those the early log builders used is nearly impossible today. The pioneer woodsmen could pick from a huge number of tree species, whereas the selection today is far more limited. The pioneers often cut their logs from slow-growing trees that consisted largely of highly decay-resistant heartwood. Furthermore, consider the size of the wood: The pioneers used virgin timber, which yielded logs 2 and 3 feet in diameter. You just can't get timber like that anymore.

Finally, consider one more salient attribute of the old logs: their charm and historic interest. Complete with bullet holes, gun ports, and dates and names carved by builders and homesteaders, these logs are vivid reminders of frontier history. The axe marks and notch work can be examined and the craftsmanship appreciated even if you are not an expert in Early Americana. The imagination comes alive. Building with logs that were hewn more than a century ago adds a special dimension to the craft—one that renders the pursuit all the more justifiable.

So salvaging logs from an old building is well worthwhile. But how does one go about the job? Very carefully. Anyone bent on restoring a log home must have a large supply of talent and time. Otherwise, the services of construction and design professionals must be procured. Just finding an appropriate cabin for restoration can be very time-consuming.

The great majority of hewn-log cabins were built in the South and in the Midwest. A survey taken in the 1930s revealed that the state of Georgia alone had 10,000 log cabins, many of them still occupied. Finding a couple of good prospects for restoration in such a region would seem easy. Like the once-ubiquitous Model A, however, the old log cabin is a vanishing commodity. Thousands still stand, but they are in such decayed condition that they no longer yield serviceable logs.

Finding a suitable cabin is often complicated by the fact that many cabins are disguised by sided-over exteriors. It was once common practice to "refine" a cabin with milled siding. This makes the cabins harder to spot. But perseverance in the search can pay off. Restorers who find these houses today are rewarded with old logs that are in like-new condition: The logs have been shielded from the weather by the siding placed over them.

The interior walls of many cabins have also been covered—the owners have applied plaster to completely conceal the logs. Only a discerning eye can spot telltale features like extra-wide window sills or door jambs: hopeful signs that beneath the plaster stands a log structure.

Once you have acquired a cabin, you can begin the process of moving it to your own land. First, you should make measured drawings and number the logs. Then the building can be dismantled. This is a dirty, dangerous, and difficult task, one best undertaken with professional aid. All the good intentions in the world won't ameliorate the impact of a 600-pound log gone awry.

Perhaps the biggest complication is that after moving a cabin, you may need to repeat the process with one or more other cabins. Since the living standards of yesterday were more modest than those of today, several cabins are usually needed to provide enough logs to form a modern home. Some of the homes featured in this chapter were forged from as many as four different log structures.

Before attempting to duplicate some of the more elaborate designs illustrated here, you should become familiar with all the processes such a project demands. Imagination and creativity are positive tools for any task, but turning old cabins into modern shelters requires solid structural and architectural sense, too. For example, planning the layout of a new structure often means working in reverse to create a floor plan that accommodates the length of the logs derived from the original cabin or cabins.

By placing modern conveniences within the framework of a reconstruction, a balance is struck between the best of old and new. Adaptive restorations become working realities through this relationship, preserving our architectural heritage while also expanding and enriching it.

MARIAH

LOCATION Free Union, Virginia • ARCHITECT (RESTORATION) Jay Dalgliesh • BUILDER (RESTORATION) Shelter Builders

Architects today are taking bold, creative license in designing adaptive restorations. No longer content with resurrecting relics of the past, architects use conventional construction and unconventional materials to produce homes of exceptional merit. Drawing on the latest ideas in building technology ensures livability, and combining these with log construction creates homes that are functionally and beautifully unique.

An example of the marriage of new technology with old building methods is found in this extraordinary home. Heat loss through the chinking is a problem that plagues many log buildings. This Achilles heel of log building was overcome here by putting a layer of stucco chinking between the logs near their exterior surfaces, then spraying insulation between the logs from the interior side, and finally putting a second layer of stucco chinking between the logs near their interior surface. In effect, this created an insulated sandwich between each pair of logs: exterior chinking, insulation, and interior chinking. According to the architect, "This made for a tighter and better-insulated cabin than we had thought possible without compromising the visual integrity of the log walls."

Indeed, as this home indicates, log construction can be highly energy efficient. By incorporating modern high-tech building materials in reconstruction, architects and builders can bring even 200-year-old log buildings into the 20th century.

(A floor plan of this house is presented at the end of the book.)

This elaborately designed door latch is as much a piece of art as it is an object of function. Such is the workmanship of days gone by — before doorknobs, keyholes, and metal bolts.

BUCKHORN

LOCATION Sevier County, Tennessee • ARCHITECT (RESTORATION) Ted Prince • BUILDER (HISTORICAL) Unknown

A naturally beautiful homesite, an imaginative mix of building materials, and an inspiring design combine to create this remarkable achievement in log building.

Is it sacrilegious to use logs in such an unconventional design? No, according to both the owner and the architect. They wanted the rustic feeling of logs without stereotypical forms. So they blended old and new styles to produce a home definitely plugged into the modern age.

For example, heating and cooling requirements are met by heat pumps. Heat is extracted from groundwater, which is then returned to a nearby stream. In summer, water from the same source is used to cool the house. This efficient,

high-tech approach to temperature maintenance is evidence of the home's unique character.

The home took extensive planning and work to build. Conceiving a pleasing blend of old and new is tricky enough. Constructing living space around an existing log building with all its door and window cutouts intact is harder still. This house is a fine example of designing in reverse: constructing a workable floor plan on the basis of an existing core structure. Such imaginative building requires ample flexibility and competence from both architect and builder.

(A floor plan of this house is presented at the end of the book.)

The living room has a strong Victorian feel, just as the owners desired. The half-moon portion of the picture window, originally from England, was mated to the fixed glass on site: an elegant contrast to the rough-hewn wall timbers.

Chestnut floor joists from an old barn are seen in the dining room and kitchen. Because of the blight that eliminated these trees from the American landscape, this rare wood is all recycled.

RIGHT: The owners follow suit in their kitchen with the rich tones of chestnut wood carried from ceiling beams to counter tops and cabinetry. It's no wonder that parties always end up in this spacious room.

MULBERRY FARM

LOCATION Purcellville, Virginia • ARCHITECT (RESTORATION) Morton Riddle IV • BUILDER (RESTORATION) Morton Riddle IV

Though the words *proportion* and *perspective* are overused in discussing architecture, they are nevertheless crucial to log-house design. Logs too big or small for the proportions of the house, windows ill-matched to wall size, and dormers dwarfing a roof are all potential pitfalls. In this house, the elements are balanced.

It is unusual to see dovetail notchings such as this around a fireplace. Yet this interesting bit of detail work adds an intriguing new element of design to the interior living room wall.

The kitchen is in the stone part of the house where the owners have placed a woodstove for heat. Today, even in the most traditional restorations, stoves often replace fireplaces for efficiency's sake.

The design uses the traditional combination of rocks and logs. In the old days, clearing a field usually produced a surplus of rocks that were often used in the parts of a house most vulnerable to weather. Also traditional is the telescoping design of this structure. Pioneers added to their

While the greenhouse may look a bit out of character for this house, the screened-in porch is both traditional and functional.

houses as their families grew: the houses expanded like unfolding telescopes.

By designing a house with a one-room-only depth, the owner of Mulberry Farm has followed other sound traditions. Minimizing the number of interior partitions between north and south walls allows better ventilation during the summer.

The owner of the house reports one problem: Expansion and contraction of wood in response to moisture fluctuations make it virtually impossible to keep the walls as airtight as they should be. Several different caulks and sealants have met with less than total success here. A last-ditch remedy would be to panel the walls. However, paneling would drastically alter the character of the house's interior.

Such a problem can be surmounted more easily during construction. A structure will be tightest if it is assembled in mild weather having low humidity and if the logs used are not too deeply checked.

STILLWATERS

LOCATION Hermann, Missouri • ARCHITECT (RESTORATION) Wheelock and Company •
BUILDER (RESTORATION) Wheelock and Company

An advertisement reading "farm with a past" first drew Sam and Lee Sammons here in 1975. At that time, there was only a ramshackle, ivy-covered farmhouse dating from the 1880s and an odd assortment of outbuildings on the property. There were no amenities to speak of—the toilet was outside and electricity was very limited.

Perfect! Inspired by tranquil surroundings and hints of a colorful past, the Sammonses bought the farm and eventually made it their permanent home. A year after purchase, as America reveled in its Bicentennial, the restoration of Stillwaters—including the construction of a substantial log addition—became the order of the day.

The addition was created by disassembling, moving, and reconstructing a two-story log cabin. Having been everything from a chicken coop to a grain warehouse, the cabin had already seen more than 150 years of American history. Even so, it was in fine shape from its center-cut, yellow pine ceiling beams to its ancient strap hinges, door locks, and window panes. In the process of restoration, nearly all these items were salvaged, so that porches and steps were the only major new components needed.

However, before the Sammons house was rightfully a home, a second building also had to be dismantled. October 2, 1848, was the date carved into the limestone chimney salvaged from this second structure.

The addition was built atop a full basement. Its marriage to the original house made room for five bedrooms, three baths, and the Sammons family of six. The surrounding acres, 250 of them, accommodate the rest of the Sammons clan—cats, dogs, songbirds, ducks, geese, catfish, and cows included!

As its name implies, this private home is surrounded by peaceful fish-filled ponds. There are two ponds on the property, both of which were man-made after the restoration of the house was completed.

LEFT: The living room is part of the log addition first built in the 1880s. Only the paneling, doors, and window frames are new.

This functionally designed railing is built to readily shed water and preserve the lower member from decay.

This bentwood willow rocker was a family heirloom handed down through the generations. Like the Stillwater restoration itself, the chair dates back to the 1800s.

The upstairs bedroom is also part of the log addition. However, the fireplace behind the tiny hand loom came from another log home where the date carved in a chimney stone reads October 2, 1848.

The grounds surrounding the Roberson homestead are lush and picturesque. The creek-side "spring house" (on following page) would make a lovely subject for its artistic owners to paint.

ROBERSON HOMESTEAD

LOCATION Townsend, Tennessee • ARCHITECT (RESTORATION) Owner • BUILDER (HISTORICAL) Unknown

Townsend, Tennessee, has a different mood from the carnival atmosphere of the nearby towns of Pigeon Forge and Gatlinburg. Like those communities, Townsend is a gateway to Great Smokies National Park, but few tourists choose this entry. So the town is much more relaxed and bucolic than its neighbors. In this pastoral setting, wildlife/landscape artists Lee and Dolores Roberson have settled. Pictured here is their art studio, a reconstructed pioneer log cabin.

The Robersons' farm is like a diorama of early East Tennessee pioneer life and history. More than just the location of a log house, the farm is a true homestead, with numerous outbuildings scattered around the grounds.

On this property, the ghosts of Boone and Crockett ambling out of the woods would come as no surprise. Yet, this is not 18th-century America and the Robersons are artists, not pioneer homesteaders. By creating a homeplace in harmony with the land's history, these artists have produced an artifact that could rival their finest paintings.

PAGE MEADOWS

LOCATION Free Union, Virginia • ARCHITECT (RESTORATION) Charles McRaven • BUILDER (RESTORATION) Charles McRaven

To become a recognized expert in a field is something many strive for but few achieve. Developing skills and acquiring knowledge takes years—few shortcuts are possible. When it comes to hand-hewn log construction and restoration, Charles McRaven is among the best. Author, blacksmith, stonemason, and log builder, McRaven has been building and restoring log homes for several decades. The double-pen house pictured here is one of his latest projects.

When the owners purchased this piece of land in Virginia, a dilapidated 16-room Victorian house was part of the deal. The home was not worth restoring in its own right, but beneath the clapboards were hewn logs. By salvaging the good logs and designing a structure to accommodate them, a solid, functional shelter was realized.

Double-pen construction, which got its name from a central wall that divided the structure into two "pens," was at one time a popular design featuring two doors for entering the house. With two doors, why not have two fireplaces? The symmetry was perfected by placing similar windows on each side of the doors. Each pen is a mirror image of the other.

The house appears to be small but is actually spacious. It includes a full basement and a sleeping loft. Though basements were unusual in pioneer times, they make good sense today since they maximize the square footage under a single roof. One advantage of building and restoring log houses in the 20th century is the availability of conveniences like premixed concrete and bulldozers. Without them, basements would be as impractical now as they were 100 years ago.

Pictured here is the saddle notch, also known as the cathedral notch because of its steeply pitched shoulders. While not as secure as the full dovetail notch, it will probably last as long.

Hand-forged door hardware and timeworn furnishings add an extra touch of realism to this restoration. Behind the chair, notch-work reveals that an interior wall divides the house in half.

POSSUM CREEK

LOCATION Charlottesville, Virginia • ARCHITECT (RESTORATION) Charles McRaven • BUILDER (RESTORATION) Charles McRaven

Like all McRaven restorations, this storybook cabin looks as if it's original to the site: No circular driveway or porte cochere, no grand entry or sweeping verandas. Just a simple, dignified cabin that melds peacefully with its setting.

Inside, living space is small but efficiently used. Combining the kitchen with the living room downstairs and the bedroom with the bath upstairs—as McRaven has done here—could produce potential inconveniences for those accustomed to more spacious surroundings. But, for those accustomed to—or willing to adapt to—a compact dwelling, it creates a cozy retreat that is easy to heat, cool, and clean.

In this compact two-story cabin, there is just enough room downstairs for a cozy living room and tiny kitchen squeezed in behind the couch and table. Yet, despite having all the amenities of any "home sweet home," the interior feels uncluttered.

CULLODEN FARM

LOCATION Gratz, Kentucky • ARCHITECT (HISTORICAL) Unknown • BUILDERS (RESTORATION) Charles and Dan McRaven

Looking much as it did when originally constructed shortly after the Civil War, this hand-hewn log home is a splendid example of a well-crafted restoration.

Its logs were hewn from white oak like the tree in the front yard. The corners were secured with V-notches, also known as saddle or cathedral notches. More than 100 years old when restoration began, the logs had been perfectly preserved by siding added shortly after the original construction. The original door and window openings were retained in the reconstruction, and much of the original limestone was salvaged to rebuild the chimneys. The front porch is one of the few features not included in the original design.

After dismantling, the entire structure was moved across the Kentucky River to the former site of a one-room schoolhouse. The farm itself was first owned by the family of John Brown, first U.S. senator from Kentucky. The current owners trace their ancestry back even further.

While structural and aesthetic authenticity are important in restorations of this sort, the practical aspects of shelter must also be considered. The Culloden farmhouse is both livable and charming. Like the white oak that shades it, this cabin should grace this spot for a long time to come.

(A floor plan of this house is presented at the end of the book.)

The warmth of a crackling fire has undeniable appeal. Sitting beside an open fireplace in a restored log farm house is like reliving a page out of a history book.

After the cabin's restoration, period furnishings were the logical choice.

RIVERVIEW

LOCATION Washington, Missouri • ARCHITECT (RESTORATION) Wheelock and Company •
BUILDER (RESTORATION) Wheelock and Company

Delving into the historical background of the structure you are restoring can be a central pleasure derived from a restoration project. Through research and insight gleaned from practice, much can be learned about the who, what, where, when, and how of the structure.

Wheelock Crosby Brown, whose firm restored this cabin, knows that it was originally built in 1820—a land-tax increase on the parcel was recorded at that time. By looking at saw marks on the boards, Brown assessed when and where they were produced. He can tell you which eras produced the various types of nails he encountered in the cabin. And he knows, for instance, that the chimney originally came from a cabin built by Daniel Boone's nephew. Brown knows these things because besides being a restoration contractor, he is also an architectural historian.

Complete reclamation of a building's history is impossible, since much information is irretrievably lost. But careful scrutiny can uncover a wealth of knowledge. Learning about a house can be at least as enjoyable as rebuilding it. Ideally, the two go hand in hand.

It took great care and thorough research to furnish this hilltop retreat with artifacts authentic to the period and nationality of its original habitants.

This picture-window porch attached to the downstairs bedroom/living area serves as an informal sunning and dining area with magnificent views across the Missouri River.

Notice the weights to the right of the fireplace. They were used like clockwork weights to help drive the rotisserie for cooking roasts and game. Today, in its original condition, the rotisserie works perfectly.

FOX GLOVE HOLLOW

LOCATION Great Smokies National Park, Tennessee • ARCHITECT (HISTORICAL) Unknown • BUILDER (HISTORICAL) Unknown

Tucked away in one of the countless "hollows" folded into Eastern Tennessee's landscape is this beautifully restored log home. It took four years to restore and exemplifies the affinity for history possessed by many residents of this part of the country. From arts and crafts to music and shelter, revival of traditional customs pervades these mountains like the mists that gave the Smokies their name.

An adaptive restoration like this is not simple, nor is it an

inexpensive alternative to modern construction. However, such preservation work is worth the toil and price, for evidence of our architectural history is rapidly vanishing.

An unusual feature of this home is the addition of the dog-trot building to the main house. Popular 150 years ago, most dog-trot cabins are now disassembled and their logs used elsewhere in restoration. By keeping the cabin intact, the owners have given themselves a pair of nice workshops—

and they also contributed to saving our architectural heritage.

The size of trees available to the pioneer log builder is demonstrated by several of the logs in the house, especially on the gable wall above the windows. The log there is wider than 2 feet and was felled and hewn with only an axe. More honest sweat was spilled in felling, shaping, and notching a few such logs than is shed in the creation of entire homes today. Recognition of such achievement is just one reward of owning a home like this.

(A floor plan of this house is presented at the end of the book.)

This interior log corner shows the half-dovetail notch, prevalent in the South since log building took hold in that region.

In the dining room as in the rest of the home, the ceiling between the timbers has been painted white. This is commonly done in log houses to brighten up the interior.

Wall logs end at the first story, then conventional framing takes over. This is apparent in the bedroom, where the rusticity of hewn timbers is replaced by the smoothness of drywall.

LAKE HOUSE

LOCATION Leeland, Michigan • ARCHITECT (RESTORATION) Jack Murchie •
BUILDERS (RESTORATION) Ray Gelter and Pete Leabo

This hewn-log home, on the northeast shore of Lake Michigan, is an adaptive restoration of unique composition. Forming the structure are three salvaged log buildings dating back to the early 1800s. The left-hand structure was originally a roadhouse from Ohio and now serves as the formal living area of the house. In the center is a tavern, also from Ohio, that forms the kitchen and dining area. On the right, rescued from imminent torching, is a former Kentucky farmhouse that is used for sleeping quarters.

Each building was too small by itself to work as a complete contemporary house, but combining them created ample living space. Piecing the three structures together was a demanding job. A good working relationship between owner, architect, and builder is needed to tackle a project of this sort. And under the best of circumstances, many tricky problems can arise.

The project architect explains:

> In our discussions, it became apparent that the authenticity pursued by the log-structure dismantler/erector did not result in terminology or techniques that coincided with current practices of the design-and-construction industry. The general contractor, who would be preparing the footings and foundations and completing the framing and finishing once the logs were erected, required verified dimensions of the log structures prior to sur-

veying, layout, and construction of the foundation walls. The dismantler/erector had dismantled two of the three buildings prior to the inception of this project and field measurements could not be made. Complicating this was the tendency of the dismantler to speak in terms of axe handles instead of feet and inches.

Though not without humor, this anecdote illustrates one difference between conventional construction and a reconstruction. This home is proof that the unconventional is possible if all players are cognizant of the pitfalls.

(A floor plan of this house is presented at the end of the book.)

The three different parts of the building have been placed at angles to reduce what would otherwise be an excessively long structure. Here, the rear of the house uses expanses of glass to yield a view of the lake.

Simply yet tastefully decorated with yesterday's furniture, the guest bedroom is located over the kitchen in the middle of the house.

The oak, beech, and poplar logs in the hallway show just how large the timbers were in the original, 18th-century log structures.

CONTEMPORARY LOG HOMES

Today, people build log homes for reasons entirely unlike those that motivated the early settlers. No longer a shelter of necessity, the log house is erected today simply because the owner chooses it. The availability of alternatives makes the decision all the more valid. In fact, the popularity of log building in this high-tech age indicates a shift in attitudes that will no doubt affect the log home's form.

Over the last decade, the log home has moved from the obscurity of the backwoods into the mainstream of American architecture. Bearing little resemblance to its frontier predecessors, today's log home is energy efficient, practical, and equipped with the amenities expected of any modern dwelling.

What started as a trickle of new log homes in recent years soon swelled to a torrent. Hundreds of log-home companies rose throughout North America to meet the demand. This explosive growth created a billion-dollar industry in little more than a decade, at a time when much of the housing industry was in a serious slump.

Legitimized, the log-building industry has split into two distinct entities: handcrafters who build with hand-hewn logs, and kit or modular log-home manufacturers, who produce log homes using modern production techniques. Since these two groups take very different approaches to log building, an examination of their respective styles is in order.

1. HAND-HEWN CONSTRUCTION. The traditional log home was constructed by felling trees, hauling logs to the house site, peeling and notching them, and assembling them into a structure. This method was used by the pioneer and is still used today. But with increased demand for log homes, a more efficient version of the hand-hewn method was needed, one that allowed increased production while retaining the hand-hewn qualities essential to log building.

Various builders responded by locating their log-building operations in areas having ample timber resources. There, they developed the off-site concept of hand-hewn log construction: Instead of traveling to a house site and creating a log home there, they produced the house at their headquarters and then shipped it to the house site.

One originator of off-site construction was Ken Thuerbach of Alpine Log Homes, in Victor, Montana. Thuerbach developed many of the techniques that ultimately made this building system viable. Consequently, Alpine Log Homes is one of the most successful companies in the business. Thuerbach conceived the idea of prebuilding a home, then dismantling it for delivery and reassembly anywhere in the country—a crucial milestone in the industry's development.

One might assume that prebuilding a log home off-site would compromise the integrity of hand-hewn construction. But in fact no quality is sacrificed. Because the houses are produced in the favorable circumstances provided by the company log yard, quality control can be assured. Moreover, prebuilding yields other advantages. For example, log homes now can be marketed in areas where timber is not readily available. Also, prebuilt log houses can be erected in locations where on-site building is difficult, such as on a hillside.

One potential disadvantage of off-site building is the owner's inability to make changes as construction progresses. You probably won't see the house while it is being produced, so you won't be able to make last-minute changes; instead, all the logs will be cut according to the design you agreed upon when ordering the house. This limitation requires careful choice of design. Significant structural changes are expensive and difficult to make once a building has been erected on site. However, this snag can be avoided by hiring a competent architect who is familiar with log construction.

Another factor to consider when ordering a handcrafted log home is that the package usually includes only the essential log shell of the structure. An on-site contractor must erect and finish the house after the logs arrive from the log company. The contractor will coordinate the activities of subcontractors, including electricians, plumbers, roofers, masons, and carpenters. Since log construction presents structural considerations not encountered in more conventional homes, it is prudent to select a contractor who is familiar with log building.

2. MODULAR CONSTRUCTION. Despite the handcrafted log industry's success, it supplies less than 15 percent of the approximately 15,000 log houses built in the United States annually. Modular or kit log-home manufacturers account for the rest.

This segment of the industry produces houses consisting of logs that have been shaped and cut to uniform dimensions, giving the manufacturer flexibility to use any log in virtually any position in the structure. Thus, the logs are not custom-cut by hand for a particular position in a particular design; rather, the logs are treated as interchangeable modules. This modular concept is both the system's strength and its weakness.

Modular log construction is conducive to mass production and consistent quality control. Production efficiency translates into lower consumer cost. And the price of a kit house contrasts favorably with that of a hand-hewn structure.

Yet cost isn't everything, and the price of uniformity is uniformity. The existence of more than 100 modular-log-home manufacturers has resulted in some repetitiveness of design that could be detrimental to the industry in the long run. An inherent trait of the log home is its unique character, and much of that individuality derives from the logs used in a building. Modular logs take on a look of sameness and so do many of the houses built with such logs. The result is what could become tract log housing.

Still, modular builders have done much to garner acceptance of log homes by both consumers and the agencies that regulate the home-building industry. A key stumbling block to the acceptance of log homes was the question of whether these homes are sufficiently energy efficient. Extensive research, funded largely by modular-log companies, proved what log-home owners already knew: Properly constructed log homes can be warmer in winter and cooler in summer than many other types of dwellings.

3. DESIGN VARIETY. More important than whether the logs used in a building are hand-hewn or modular is the style of the building itself. A box is still a box no matter

what kind of logs compose it. The pioneer used logs to build simple houses, but the modern-day log builder is not required to follow suit. Log construction is a construction technique, not an architectural style. So, log building can harness almost any design to create harmony between structure and components.

This chapter, like the previous one, demonstrates that combining logs with other materials enlarges the parameters of log design to encompass diverse architectural styles. Many of the houses used as examples herein resist categorical labeling. Much innovative design can be attributed to a new breed of architects and builders unfettered by the chains of tradition. By using modern, state-of-the-art building materials in conjunction with logs, they have created truly new designs that are simultaneously extremely sturdy structures.

What of the future of log building? Is log construction a fad, as skeptics insist, or will it continue to flourish? The answer lies in logs' viability as a building material.

At present, log homes consume a very small percentage of our forest resources. Unless the industry's growth rate surges phenomenally, its impact on timber resources will remain minimal. And, as other building materials are used in conjunction with logs, even fewer trees will be needed.

Supplies of timber almost surely will not determine the future of log building; rather, the controlling factor will be the availability of human resources. The demand for log homes will continue so long as architects and builders respond to homebuyers' needs. How well they respond will shape, to a large degree, the future of the log-building industry. We hope that the structures illustrated in this book will offer inspiration to help perpetuate the American Log Home.

KONA MEADOWS

LOCATION Hailey, Idaho • ARCHITECT Bob Reese • BUILDERS Steve Mantey, Jake Lemmon, and Tom Blanchard

Located just north of Hailey, Idaho, this handcrafted log house is the manifestation of a dream and six years of hard work. Owner Bob Reese designed the house, then brought the intricate structure to life with the capable help of several local craftsmen.

Working with limited building experience, Reese first constructed a model from his plans. This is a good approach, and one not limited to neophyte builders. Many architects erect models of untested designs to see how well they work.

Changes are easier to make with a quarter-inch dowel than with a log weighing several hundred pounds!

Upon completion of the model, ground was broken and the real structure erected, following the model virtually log for log—or log for dowel. The basic design is a two-story shed with a clerestory, wedded to a five-sided single-story structure under a roof of seven planes. Obviously, with such a complex design, it was indeed prudent to construct a model first.

LEFT: This junction of rafters, plate logs, and posts converging at a corner of the front porch roof is a tricky yet eye-catching piece of joinery—from the bird's point of view as well!

It was no easy task finding a living room couch to fit the concave form of the kitchen counter. In front, the sunken fireplace keeps splinters and ashes out of the carpet.

LEFT: The owner, who built this home, first created a model so that roof angles and complicated support systems could be more easily calculated. The dining area shown here sits to the rear of the house.

PANTHER PLACE

LOCATION Sawtooth Mountains, Idaho • ARCHITECTS William Ware and Ralph Rutter • BUILDER Rutter Construction

From snow-capped mountains to charred lava fields and lush bottom lands, south-central Idaho offers extreme contrasts. It is also actively affected by the restless forces of nature. Though surrounding volcanoes have long been silent, residents must still contend with floods, avalanches, and earthquakes. That this area is one of the most seismically active in the continental United States was a fact the owners of this log home did not ignore.

Architect/builder Ralph Rutter designed and erected this robust structure using sawn logs in conjunction with post-and-beam framing. The emphasis on structural integrity is evident throughout the building, but interesting design elements are also present. A hip-roofed wing reduces the building's otherwise imposing height. Subsequent cantilevering of the wing made the design balanced rather than ponderous.

Daring in concept, the cantilevered section was carefully designed, engineered, and built to ensure minimal settling. The heavy superstructure and potential snow loads of 150 pounds per square foot necessitated strong underpinnings that would resist deflection.

Sawn logs will stack flat, but the owners wanted the traditional chinked look. After three-inch planks were placed between the wall logs, a chinking mixture of Portland cement and sand was applied. This unorthodox approach to building with sawn logs is only one of many features that make this home unique.

(A floor plan of this house is presented at the end of the book.)

By cantilevering bulky timbered floor joists out over the walls of its river rock foundation, the architect has made this sturdy structure less ponderous.

Panther Place is pure muscle inside and out. Everything is large, yet built nicely to scale—an important consideration when designing or furnishing any home. Because this home sits on a steep hillside, it incorporates as many as four levels of living space.

This balcony office overlooks the dining room below. Amazingly, the forward part of the balcony hangs freely without the need for awkward posts holding it up from below. It is instead supported from above by hefty trusses reinforced with dozens of metal truss-plate connectors.

ARROW RANCH

LOCATION Big Hole Basin, Montana • ARCHITECT David Lorimer • BUILDER Mountain Log Homes

This log home commands a solitary view of the Big Hole Basin of Montana. Although its design may seem incongruous in this land of sprawling ranches and sparse tree cover, its presence here is testimony to the diversity of log architecture.

The architect downplayed the building's prominence on the hill by designing the roof in broad planes that conform with the austere lines of the landscape. The overall effect is a building hugging the land. Viewed from a distance, the hipped roof blends surprisingly well with the surrounding mountains and further diminishes any sense that the structure is out of place.

The home's interior feels expansive. An abundance of glass fills the home with natural light and affords grand vistas of the outlying land.

The terrain here is often referred to as "that awesome space," a term that can lead some people to overbuild or overdesign in response to the environment. The opposite tack was taken here to blend rather than dominate.

(A floor plan of this house is presented at the end of the book.)

Standing before the fireplace, you can see the dining room and kitchen extending beyond the sunken living room. Though not very evident in this photo, the glass wall in the foreground is a short cantilevered bay.

This living room displays creative evidence of its owner's hobby. The room sports a wide variety of record-book animal trophies from around the world. The fireplace decor is rare indeed!

NORTHWOOD

LOCATION Ketchum, Idaho • ARCHITECT Janet Jarvis • BUILDERS Peter Dembergh, Ashley Gilbert, and Custom Log Homes

As architects become increasingly involved in the construction of log houses, traditional forms give way to more contemporary designs. This passive-solar house is a case in point.

Designed by an architect specializing in log homes, the house uses both post-and-beam and horizontal-log construction.

To take advantage of solar potential, the architect placed large glass areas in the southern walls. By using two-story post-and-beam construction, she was able to create the necessary window openings while maintaining structural integrity. Minimizing the amount of wood used in this section also decreased the likelihood of glass breakage when moisture fluctuations cause log movement.

A hindrance to wider acceptance of log houses as primary residences is the stereotype of them as vacation homes or rural dwellings. But as this house shows, log houses today can well reflect modern life-styles.

(A floor plan of this house is presented at the end of the book.)

Extensive glazing opens up southward views and is receptive to the rays of the sun. Illumination is even throughout most of this home, due in part to the high reflectivity of the ceilings.

An entry such as this, which doubles as a "cold room," is especially practical where mountain-town winters last up to seven months. The front door is closed to the frosty winds before the main house is entered through interior French doors.

A soothing hot tub sits "kitty-corner" to the living room. As seen in the overall exterior photo of this home, the glass panels of the solarium rise two stories high to fully utilize the simple technique of heating with sunshine.

BEAVER SPRINGS

LOCATION Ketchum, Idaho • ARCHITECT Thadd Blanton • BUILDER Mountain Log Homes

"Charming" is a term often used to describe log homes. Both subjective and objective factors contribute to this quality. The house shown here has an abundance of charm.

The setting of the home plays an important role. Situated under the canopy of several large cottonwoods, the house seems to have grown from the site. Extra effort in excavation and building was needed to prevent injury to the trees, but the result was worth the trouble.

Notice how the decks and the house seem to emerge directly from the ground. A close harmony is established

The entry stairway's squared-off posts and ornamental crowns stand in stark contrast to rounded log walls and cylindrical ceiling joists. However, this sawn-lumber addition, balanced somewhat by the heavy deacon's bench across the hall, works especially well.

with the earth. The effect is visually pleasing and practical as well. Because building codes dictate minimum separation between wood and dirt, naturally decay-resistant woods or pressure-treated lumber must be used in such a design.

The river-rock chimney contributes greatly to the beauty of the house. Although the exposed chimney is a liability from an energy efficiency standpoint, it imparts a strong traditional flavor, which in turns creates that elusive quality called charm.

Last but not least are the logs. After years of oiling and exposure to the sun, they have taken on a warm color. Mellowing with age, log homes often become more beautiful with the passing years.

(A floor plan of this house is presented at the end of the book.)

The steeply pitched ceilings in the upstairs master bedroom are loftlike in design but hardly cramped—there is ample living space. This shot shows only half the room. Note that the ceilings are extremely high.

AVALANCHE RANCH

LOCATION East Fork Canyon, Idaho • ARCHITECT David A. Schlechten • BUILDERS Allan Blair, Ike Kola, and Mountain Log Homes

On a watermelon afternoon in high summer, the name Avalanche Ranch seems anomalous for this sturdy log house. Yet, summers in central Idaho give way all too soon to heavy winter snows. Temperatures drop to -30°F and avalanches roar down the chutes that line the canyon walls.

On February 25, 1917, one such slide struck the North Star Mine, located not far from here. Descending without warning at 3:30 A.M., it killed 17 miners and in-

jured 17 more. The event serves today as a grim reminder that mountain snows mean more than pleasant skiing in fresh powder.

Deep winter snows can place extreme loads on roofs. Here, the architect has designed a purlined roof system to withstand the storms. The structural advantage of purlins over rafters is their ability to transfer roof loads to the gable walls as a vertical force. With rafters, the loads are transferred to

eave walls, tending to thrust outward. The thrust can be counteracted by adding other elements to the rafter design, but purlin construction—simple and strong—is often a better choice.

Another good design element for snow country is the sheltered entry. By recessing the entry, the architect has protected this area from falling and blowing snow. Although they would seem necessary for houses in winter climes, such entries are seen too rarely.

(A floor plan of this house is presented at the end of the book.)

Arched entryways are especially popular with Canadian log builders. Artistic log designs flourish on both sides of the United States-Canada border.

In the kitchen, creative brickwork hides the woodburning stove, the "cook counter," and the ovens.

It's no wonder how this ranch, in Idaho snow country, got its name. Historically, fatal avalanches have occurred all too frequently.

STANDING BEAR LODGE

LOCATION Sawatch Mountains, Colorado • ARCHITECTS Steve Cappellucci and owner • BUILDER Steve Cappellucci

Many ingredients contribute to a successful building project, but none is more important than the builder. In the case of Standing Bear Lodge, that distinction belongs to Steve Cappellucci of Almont, Colorado.

Drawing upon his extensive log and wood joinery experience, Cappellucci handcrafted this house with logs from the surrounding forests. Discontent with more familiar and simpler styles of building, he chose to craft the corners of

Wallpaper and brightly patterned fabrics immerse this child's bedroom in fresh, lively color. What little girl could resist?

This extraordinary house with its distinctive bay uses dovetail notching and "skip-peeled" logs having some of the bark left on for color and texture.

the building with intricate dovetail notches. Cappellucci taught himself the techniques as he worked.

With a creative flair for woodworking, Cappellucci designed and built many distinctive features for this home. From hammer beam trusses to furniture, and from cabinets to windows, his craftsmanship is evident throughout the structure: a truly outstanding example of the handcrafted log home.

LEFT: *Although high over head, this arched truss becomes the focal point of the room. While not a true hammer beam truss because it uses a steel rod cross tie, it is a clever design.* ABOVE: *The kitchen counter serves to divide living and dining areas. Note the use of flat and full logs in this sun-drenched room. When the room gets warm, shades cover the upper windows.*

BROOKBEAR LODGE

LOCATION Glenbrook, Nevada • ARCHITECT Arthur Hannafin • BUILDER Hannafin Construction

The popularity of log building in the early development of America was due in large part to the availability of abundant, free building materials. Construction was simple, the results sturdy, and, in most cases, the trees had already been felled to create farmland. The log house was a structure of necessity, dictated by the times and the environment rather than by aesthetics. Things are different now. This modern, twin-gambrel–roofed home was built as an expression of individuality, a quality as important as practicality today.

Using milled logs for this house, the builder and architect achieved a rustic appearance without struggling to execute natural, full-log construction. The ten-inch cedar logs were

The premise behind the home was that log structures are not confining. It's a matter of understanding the integrity of the structure, then just having fun. Every room here shines with personality.

The owners of this home decorated the various bedrooms in markedly different styles. This room has feminine touches that soften the "masculinity" of logs and stone.

milled in such a way that they form weathertight joints without chinking. The logs were individually notched at the building site instead of at the log yard, so that the builder and architect could make changes during construction.

Located on the northeastern shore of Lake Tahoe, the house was built in an area rich in early Tahoe history. From here, logs cut in the surrounding forests were flumed thousands of feet down to Virginia City, where they were used to shore up the silver mines of the late 1800s. Directly below the house, in what are now lush meadows known as China Gardens, Chinese mill workers grew vegetables in their camps. It seems fitting to locate a log home in an area where the forest played such an important historic role.

LEADVILLE

LOCATION Ketchum, Idaho • ARCHITECTS Ruscitto, Latham and Blanton • BUILDERS Steve Riley and Peter Dembergh

The proliferation of sawmills throughout the western United States had a twofold effect on log building: Logs were fashioned with two sides or replaced altogether with sawn lumber. The two-sided log was a popular building material in Idaho's Wood River Valley during the 1930s, and it still has its place today.

Built-in bunk beds maximize space in the children's room, especially when combined with drawers placed underneath.

One attraction of building with sawn logs is the ease with which they can be fitted tightly without chinking. This home is a good example of this building approach.

More than 40 log courses high, the home is unusually tall for a log structure. Also unusual, but gaining in popularity, is the use of post-and-beam framing principles along with the conventional stacking of logs. By using post-and-beam techniques, the architect expanded the glass areas within the walls and partially eliminated the repetitious effect of projecting log ends.

The roof is supported by triple log purlins that provide ample support for heavy snow loads. In addition, the architect wisely chose to use triple fascia boards and a large Boston ridge to give the roof more dimension. Covering

such a large structure, a roof of ordinary design would have lacked proper proportions.

One design element is arguably out of proportion. The chimney's projection through the roof might have been made several feet higher, though height limitations might have precluded it.

(A floor plan of this house is presented at the end of the book.)

Plaster-and-stucco ceilings and walls brighten the rooms of this house while contrasting with the logs.

WOOD ACRES

LOCATION Wilson, Wyoming • ARCHITECTS (DESIGNERS) Kenneth and Carol Wood • BUILDER Jim Budge

One persistent stigma attached to log houses is that they tend to be dark. This may have been true in pioneer days, but it's hardly the case now. To take advantage of spectacular views of the Teton Range, this house features vast expanses of glass.

Before constructing a house with so much glass, you should take steps to offset some potential drawbacks. Of primary concern is the loss of heat through the glass. Even double

and triple glazing allow much heat to escape at night unless the windows are fitted with insulating shades, curtains, or shutters.

Another consideration is structural integrity. Because glass has very little strength, caution must be exercised in designing a home having large expanses of glass. You must make sure that roof loads are adequately transferred to the foundation; none of the loads should bear on the windows themselves.

A view of Wyoming's Grand Tetons greets the eye from this dramatic wall of windows. Impressive inside is the center-post construction.

Another problem often overlooked is birds colliding with large windows. A bird can easily mistake clear glass for the wild blue yonder—with shattering results. Sturdy tempered glass is one solution.

Large glass windows present potential problems, but they also confer great advantages. Awareness of potential trouble will enable the builder to plan accordingly and will keep the home filled with both natural light and views of the great outdoors.

(A floor plan of this house is presented at the end of the book.)

Inspired by their surroundings, the owners designed this colorful front entry, treating it as if it were a piece of art.

SUMMIT HOUSE

LOCATION East Fork Canyon, Idaho • ARCHITECT John Daley • BUILDER Dennis Kavanagh and Mountain Log Homes

It is often said that the location of a house is its most important attribute. This homesite supports the claim. The balcony off the upstairs master bedroom commands a view of a rushing river, looming mountains, and lush vegetation. What a fine sight to wake up to in the morning—what an excellent site for a log house!

The design features two shed additions flanking a central two-story structure. The living room is centrally located on the first floor with guest bedrooms on the left and dining and kitchen facilities on the right. Entrances to both the living area and the kitchen off the deck are used extensively during the summer.

This handcrafted bed faces French doors and the river beyond. At its headboard, behind the planter, is an open master bathroom.

Opposite the living room are the kitchen and compact dining area. An ample, wraparound deck is accessible from all three rooms.

Seen from the kitchen, this well-lit living room is nicely framed by an expansive archway. Its bright stucco fireplace goes well with logs.

The roof is constructed with purlins that support the decking. A thoughtful feature of the roof design is the way runoff is directed to the sides of the building, where occupants are least affected. Many roof designs ignore such considerations.

(A floor plan of this house is presented at the end of the book.)

SADDLE RIDGE

LOCATION Sun Valley, Idaho • ARCHITECT Darryl McMillen • BUILDERS John Lloyd and Mountain Log Homes

Many factors must be considered when building or buying a log home. Some are frivolous, like, "Will I be able to hang pictures on a log wall?" Others, like the fire resistance of log structures, are quite important. This example addresses the latter concern.

Within days of completion, this imposing log home's fire resistance was inadvertently tested. An oil-soaked rag discarded on Friday led, through spontaneous combustion, to a fire that went unnoticed over the weekend. Contained to a small area around the front entry, the fire finally broke

Though small, the kitchen is well laid-out. With hand-painted tiles, rough textured stucco walls, and "vigas" extending out above the cabinets, the southwestern flavor is unmistakable.

through to the outside. A passing jogger saw the flames and notified the fire department. The blaze was extinguished before serious damage resulted.

The fire's spread was minimal because it took so long to burn through the 16-inch-thick logs. Damage was limited to a three-foot section that burned next to the front door. Converting the entry from a single- to double-door entry eliminated the flame scar and simultaneously improved the design.

Reduced flame spread is only one advantage of logs when a fire occurs. More important is the fact that burning wood emits fewer toxic fumes than conventional walls—especially walls containing plastic vapor barriers. Wall coverings (paneling, paint, vinyl wallpaper) can also make a difference. Because toxic fumes often lead to fire fatalities, this difference is very significant.

(A floor plan of this house is presented at the end of the book.)

When a construction fire burned through the wall next to the front entry, builders simply changed plans to accommodate double doors.

STRAWBERRY PARK

LOCATION Steamboat Springs, Colorado • ARCHITECT Owner • BUILDER John Beauregard

Families often build small houses, then add new living space to suit their needs, fancies, or pocketbooks. This house is a case in point. It began small and then evolved into a larger structure.

When builder John Beauregard started building this log house for Vincent and Virginia Grillo, he constructed the section with the gambrel roof. The logs in this section are squared on three sides while the fourth retains its bark: a log-building style common to Colorado's Yampa Valley. Simple in design, the original structure had the casual feel of a country home. It was pleasant, but it hardly reflected the owners' energetic life-style and eclectic tastes. Over time, Beauregard's successful interpretation of the family's

The kids are gone, but when they return the gang gathers here. Less formal than the rest of the house is this combination of family room, informal dining nook, and—the family's favorite—the kitchen.

desires resulted in several well-crafted additions that gave the home a dramatic new image.

A spacious kitchen was added, along with more living space. Later, an office took the form of a turret. Here, short log sections are skillfully mitered end-to-end to create a circular form. The turret interrupts the linear forms in the house and balances the original structure. Finally, the addition of a greenhouse completed the transformation of the home.

The turret serves as an office and sitting area. The multiple rafters are tied to a common king post overhead. Beyond the drawn curtains is an uncluttered view of the pond and valley.

WINDEMERE

LOCATION Blaine County, Idaho • ARCHITECT John Gudmundsson • BUILDER John Gudmundsson

In using logs for the first-floor walls and conventional framing for the roof and gable ends, the owner/builder of this home was able to combine the best features of both approaches.

Much time and effort can be saved by using dimensioned lumber instead of logs in a roof structure. With the consistency of sawn-lumber rafters, cuts can be duplicated quickly and accurately, whereas with unmilled logs, each rafter must be crafted individually. In addition, because roof systems are so important structurally, it is sometimes easier to get house plans approved by skeptical building officials when the roof is built to specifications they are familiar with. This is not to say that log-roof systems are inadequate by any means, but given the proclivity of some building officials to say no, it may be wise to give yourself the option of a conventional roof.

In this country charmer, high ceilings, glass, and greenery bring the outside in. Three-sided logs give the appearance of rough paneled walls. While this is certainly a legitimate building style, heating can be a problem if the logs are shaved too thin.

The master bedroom is tucked into a spacious upstairs loft. The owner opted for a conventionally framed roof versus one framed with logs.

In this house, the upper story could have been framed in logs. This would have carried the log effect to the roof, where the separation of the two forms would be expected. The decision to make the transition lower—at the base of the second-floor walls—adds an interesting element to the home's design.

BALDWIN RANCH

LOCATION Alta, Wyoming • BUILDER Rex Christiansen

Originally designed for log-and-frame construction, this house withstood numerous design changes before being built with logs. Builder Rex Christiansen handcrafted the house on the site, using logs from the surrounding mountains.

Christiansen's first log project, the house took three years to complete. But Christiansen wasn't daunted by the job. He created another log house, a log barn, and a 15-acre lake as parts of the same project: a formidable task indeed!

The living room hosts a plethora of wild game mounts and handcrafted furniture. Knobby wood and antler chandeliers add exciting textures to this colorful space.

Distinguishing the house's exterior design are the extended gables that cover the porch and entry. Gables must be well supported to resist snow loads in this part of the country, and the necessary underpinnings can easily clutter the exterior. By using trusses and extended wall logs, the home works well with a minimum of posts.

Also worth noting are the irregular logs used for posts. The logs came from lodgepole forests that were infected with parasitic diseases. As the trees fought infection, they grew around the affected areas to form intriguing shapes.

Not shown here is a two-story turret facing the lake at the rear of the home. Constructed with vertical logs, the turret encloses the dining area. Vertical logs also frame the dormers, offering contrast for the horizontal-log walls. Such mixes of design elements have transformed the simple log cabin of yesterday into the beautiful log home of today.

Here's a bathroom playfully decorated in the image of an elegant old western cat house. With its overhead-flush commode and clawfoot bathtub, the only thing missing is a cowboy, a beautiful woman, and a bubble bath.

Along with the western motif is an impressive display of contemporary log work. Here rafters meeting the walls are exposed to reveal mortise-and-tenon notches. Also note the bay window seat design.

Palisaded logs carried up through the master bedroom from below are part of a turret built onto the rear of the house. The use of vertical logs in this way adds a distinctive touch to the design.

RUSHING WATERS

LOCATION Zinc Spur, Idaho • ARCHITECT Helen Ziegler • BUILDERS Sawtooth Construction and Mountain Log Homes

Set beside the snow-filled channels of the Wood River in south-central Idaho, the home of Mark and Penny Brown is a picture of pastoral tranquility. Not too long ago, however, the scene was very different—circumstances threatened the very existence of this attractive structure.

Snow fell early in the high country during the winter of 1983-84. By midwinter, the mountain snow pack was 150 percent above normal—a harbinger of serious spring flooding. With the bulk of the snow pack still intact in May, the potential for high water was alarming.

Five days of unusually hot temperatures produced massive runoff into the river. The floodplain became a plain flood. Huge cottonwood trees tumbled into the river, their rootballs dragging along the river bed and creating vibrations felt along the banks. Dump trucks roared up and down the valley 24 hours a day, carrying rock from abandoned silver mines with which to reinforce the river banks.

As the river began cutting a new channel toward the house, the owners took action. In a last-ditch effort to save their home, they placed tons of rock along the rapidly eroding upstream bank. The plan worked and the house was saved at what may well have been the last moment.

(A floor plan of this house is presented at the end of the book.)

In the kitchen and throughout the house, care was taken to give the logs a warm appearance. Each was washed with a bleach solution, then coated with several layers of orange shellac.

This bold design is strengthened by a floor plan commanding visual access from one room to the next. From the living room couch, the owners can see the entry, mind the pots boiling on the stove, watch the kids playing in the loft, and glimpse the sun setting outside the dining room windows.

The rounded baylike portion of this home makes a pleasant dining area. A curving row of picture windows permits a panoramic view of winter in Idaho. This corner room, built with log posts, is paneled inside while the outside is faced with river rock.

SILVER QUEEN

LOCATION Park City, Utah • ARCHITECT (DESIGNER) Nancy McComb • BUILDERS Alpine Log Homes and owner

During its silver boomtown days, Park City burgeoned with construction. But when the price of silver fell and the mines started to play out, the town went bust like so many other western communities.

Park City was reborn through the discovery that as much money could be made atop a mountain as inside one. The ski industry now brings more money into the community than was ever extracted in silver. Today's high-grade ore is

a two-foot snowstorm that in days gone by would have produced only curses from miners.

Perched on a knoll outside Park City is this tri-level, six-bedroom, five-bath log house. The design of such a large house demands careful avoidance of a barnlike appearance. By angling two wings from a central core, the designer has visually reduced this house, while retaining the actual square footage needed for a large family. Wraparound decks permit outdoor access to various portions of the house.

A glance at the lookalike condominiums nearby succinctly tells why people today are choosing distinctive building styles. Upon returning home, the inhabitants of this house are not likely to enter their neighbor's door in a case of mistaken identity.

The sole log spanning the living room serves as a tie between the walls and is essential to the structural soundness of the building.

A great deal of energy went into the landscaping of the Silver Queen. Here, tons of local rock, laboriously maneuvered into position, form a retaining wall against the slope—they are a fitting seat for the stairway.

INDEPENDENCE CREEK

LOCATION Sun Valley, Idaho • ARCHITECT David A. Schlechten • BUILDERS Custom Log Homes and Tom Denker

The doors in this master bedroom lead out to a deck that is equipped with a hot tub. Outdoor stairs also lead to the tub from below, giving guests convenient access.

Taken away from the forest, the log house still melds with its setting, even if in many instances contrast is apparent. In the sagebrush-covered hills of central Idaho, this design fits well with the landscape, even though the only trees to be found are new plantings.

Among the features of this home that help it fit in with its surroundings are the roof lines that match the hills beyond, providing an elusive tie to the land. Add a sod roof, and environmental assimilation is complete.

By offsetting the garage from the main house, the architect has created the illusion of a detached garage. Though the benefits of attaching a garage to a home are many and obvious, the blending of the two structures is rarely harmonious, especially in log plans.

(A floor plan of this house is presented at the end of the book.)

Although seldom used, the dining room has its own fireplace that shares a common chimney with the living room on the other side and master bedroom above. To the right, between the kitchen and dining areas, French doors lead to the step-up solarium.

The interior design of this home, having something of a Spanish flavor, incorporates arched fireplaces with inlaid tile, wicker, greenery, and plenty of stucco. On the balcony, the central fireplace continues upward, hiding only the master bed. The space to each side remains open.

WILD TURKEY RIDGE

LOCATION Steamboat Springs, Colorado • ARCHITECT John Beauregard • BUILDER John Beauregard

The intriguing half-log bench and mitered window detailing exemplify the craftsmanship that went into this home.

A hobbit-style stairway with polished half-log treads and solid, bentwood railings is truly one of a kind.

Situated on a hillside with the ski runs of Mount Werner as a backdrop, this intriguing house is a fine example of builder John Beauregard's log-building expertise. Expanding on the sawn-log building style prevalent in this part of Colorado, Beauregard has created a very distinctive design.

For example, the triangulated glass in the gable end not only breaks the uniformity of the log walls but adds much-needed light. The Gothic arch, a Beauregard hallmark, supplements both door and window treatments. Bending logs to this shape is impossible, so he carefully sections each timber to attain the curves. By mitering pieces of the same log, he retains continuity of grain and other wood characteristics, thus heightening the illusion of a curved log.

While the exteriors of Beauregard's houses are unique examples of log building, the interiors best showcase his talents. Treating interior structural elements like pieces of furniture, he designs and builds his houses so no two are alike. This house required many hours of searching the forest for just-right pieces of wood, plus many more hours fitting them together. The result speaks for itself.

(A floor plan of this house is presented at the end of the book.)

ROLLING J RANCH

LOCATION Colorado Rockies • ARCHITECTS John Beauregard and owner • BUILDER John Beauregard

In designing for his clients, John Beauregard has achieved excellent results by using some unorthodox methods. Inspired by architecture from places as far away as Thailand and South America, Beauregard and his client drew the design for this home on a grocery bag one afternoon.

Using a mixture of arches, angles, and geometric shapes—hallmarks of his creations—Beauregard designed another one-of-a-kind home. And then, because he is no armchair architect content to turn over his designs to construction contractors, he proceeded to build the home himself.

His unique designs may not suit everybody's tastes, but it's refreshing to see an artist take log construction beyond the realm of the ordinary.

The builder of this house is a true craftsman, paying careful attention to detail with unending patience. By mitering together numerous sections of wood, he can achieve nearly any shape desired.

Though nearly new, the house wears its decor with the dignity of age. The mood is highlighted by backlit stained-glass windows and ancient barnwood siding.

LEFT: Upstairs, a short balcony walkway separates two large bedrooms. Once again, we see the incredible design potential of mitered logs. ABOVE: The kitchen fits into an elongated bay, where ceiling rafters extend from a common king post in the center. Separating this room from the main living area is this double-width countertop affixed to a massive river-rock base.

BEYOND HOPE

LOCATION Hope, Idaho • BUILDERS Jim Carhart and Mountain Log Homes

The summer residence of Klaus Groenke of West Germany, this house is reminiscent of European design. With an extended roof gable and a full-width balcony, the home is like a chalet, a building type found throughout central and northern Europe.

Readily apparent, even at a distance, is the immense size of the logs used in construction. They have midspan diameters averaging 2 feet or more. When using logs on this scale, several factors must be considered. First, such logs come from nearly mature trees, so heart rot may be pres-

ent. This is a natural condition of old age in trees, and the decay can be spotted easily.

Second, most door and window units are not designed for 2-foot-thick walls. Fabricating custom jambs and/or windows and doors solves the problem, albeit expensively.

The kitchen and dining areas are on one side of this large central fireplace while the living room is on the other. Notice the distinctive stone work that frames the fireplace's mouth.

For this outdoor stairway, the builders took an unusual approach to tread design. Because the treads were attached with pegs instead of nails, a damaged tread can be easily unfastened and replaced.

Finally, the building must be scaled to the size of the logs. Designs for 6-inch-thick walls translate into rooms ill-suited for logs four times thicker. Because log walls tend to shrink a room visually, you need to compensate for oversize logs.

Keeping such points in mind can ensure that a large-log home will please its inhabitants for many years.

EAGLE CREEK RANCH

LOCATION Eagle Creek, Idaho • ARCHITECTS Ruscitto, Latham and Blanton • BUILDER Dave Carter

Logs squared on two sides mimic post-and-beam design, and they allow the use of many large, closely set windows in this tri-level home.

With the owner's penchant for riding, roping, and training quarter horses, life on this ranch revolves around the attractive log barn.

Following the trend away from using logs exclusively, this contemporary home incorporates conventional framing and rocks as well as logs in its design. Especially interesting is the blending of rocks and logs in the garage wall.

The deck recessed in the roof is a nice feature, offering a well-protected and private sunning area. It also provides light for the kitchen. There is a question, however, about what to do with the snow that accumulates there in winter.

The addition of a translucent canopy over the area would create a fine solarium and add much to the house's livability.

Besides the house, the ranch has an architecturally harmonious log-and-frame barn. The original owner raised and trained cutting horses, so a functional barn was necessary. It features a hayloft, horse stalls, and caretaker's quarters.

(A floor plan of this house is presented at the end of the book.)

MEDICINE SPRINGS

LOCATION Steamboat Springs, Colorado • ARCHITECT Chris Shaw • BUILDER Chris Shaw

When Chris Shaw decided to build log houses, he sought formal training in the craft—he signed up for a log building course taught by veteran log builder Krissa Johnson of Lake Placid, New York. What Shaw didn't realize at the time was that Johnson was leading an all-female class.

The mistake went undiscovered until class sessions began, and by then it was too late to change his plans. As it turned out, however, Shaw got along well with his 17 classmates and learned a lot about log building. He returned to Colorado and built this, his first hand-hewn log house. Perched high on a mountainside overlooking the Yampa Valley, the home would have been quite an undertaking for a seasoned log builder. For a first-timer like Shaw, it is a remarkable achievement.

The overall design is simple: a two-story gabled structure with a one-story shed. Balancing the main building are a garage and an airlock entry. The garage was excavated so its doors are lower than the level of the main house. Visually, this separates the garage doors from the rest of the house—always a good point of design. The gabled dormer over the garage brings light to the living area above the garage and serves to keep snow and runoff from unloading in front of the doors.

One enters this home from the left—passing through a solar greenhouse next to the living room. Inside, the logs were purposely left dark because the owner finds the effect soothing and warm.

A direct view across the living room from the greenhouse reveals this unusual scalloped entryway—an interesting departure from the more common, smooth-arched entries shown elsewhere.

WHISPERING PINES

LOCATION Bitterroot Valley, Montana • ARCHITECT Scott Pickels • BUILDER Alpine Log Homes

During 200 years of American log building, the essential construction principles have remained the same. Logs are still laid horizontally with corner notching to hold them in place. Recent years, however, have seen the incorporation of new auxiliary technologies in log homes. An example is this house located near Victor, Montana.

When the owners looked to the sun and the woods to heat their house, they knew traditional approaches would not suffice in this very cold climate. So they opted for a sophisticated solar greenhouse. Heat from the greenhouse moves into the home through large French doors. Additional heat

There is nothing like a wood cookstove to create nostalgia for days gone by. This old Monarch, still in perfect working order, continues to age gracefully in the setting built especially for it.

During the long, harsh winter, dining in the greenhouse is a delight. However, in summer, screening sunlight out becomes important. For this purpose, operable shutters have been installed overhead.

The owners took special care with the kitchen layout so that the living room would be visible from the kitchen counter. It's no fun to cook alone.

A huge, four-car garage with an upstairs recreation area and guest quarters stands separate from the main house. In this case, covered walkways are almost a necessity due to heavy winter snows.

is stored for use after the sun sets: Hot air from near the roof of the greenhouse is blown through pipes buried in a rock heat-storage area. The rocks absorb the heat, then later release it slowly to help keep the home warm around the clock. The greenhouse is equipped with insulating shutters and shades to prevent heat loss through the glass when the sun is down.

The home also has an airtight woodstove that is equipped with a water jacket. When the greenhouse is unable to provide as much heat as the home needs, the woodstove is lit and water is circulated through the jacket. The heated water is then sent through a second set of pipes buried in the rock heat-storage area, replenishing the rocks' supply of heat.

As this home shows, new approaches and new products can make today's log house fully as up to date as any other dwelling.

(A floor plan of this house is presented at the end of the book.)

According to the owners, when they designed their house, all they really wanted was a kitchen and a four-car garage. But the combined living room and dining area they created is certainly a joy. The atmosphere is open and friendly.

Not only is the greenhouse an enjoyable area in this home, but it is designed to be an integral part of this home's unique heating system. Solar heat gathered by the greenhouse is distributed throughout the home.

A spacious recreation room sits above the garage. Next to this room is a large, separate apartment. For complete privacy, the shelf above the rec-room counter swings down and locks shut.

This compact den is situated in the upstairs dormer, the design of which is particularly interesting. Cantilevered logs are used as a partial support system for valley rafters, an unusual structural approach.

CEDAR PLACE

LOCATION Missoula, Montana • ARCHITECT Wilbur Watkins • BUILDER Wilbur Watkins

When Wilbur "Bunts" Watkins decided to build a log house to celebrate the 25th anniversary of his marriage, he decided to do it up big. Fulfilling a boyhood dream of building with logs is not uncommon, but doing it on such a grand scale certainly is. These logs, some more than 3 feet in diameter, are huge.

Building with such large timbers presents tough problems, like the inability to cut notches in the logs for the corners of

the structure. Watkins circumvented this by mitering the ends of the logs used at the corners. This technique is occasionally used. It is easier, but less sturdy: Strength is sacrificed without the interlocking effect of notching. To at least partially compensate for the loss of sturdiness, the logs are fastened together along their length with steel pins or dowels.

Another distinction of this home is the retention of bark on

the logs. While imparting a rustic look and slightly increasing the insulation value of the logs, the bark comes with some inherent problems. The fragile nature of the bark requires careful handling. In addition, bark is often host to insects that can make housecleaning difficult.

A bright white door accentuates the massive, unpeeled cedar logs used in the first story of this distinctive home.

Elegant stairway railings came from the old Broadwater Inn in Helena, Montana. Here they stand in notable contrast to rough-barked cedar.

BEARTOOTH

LOCATION Hamilton, Montana • ARCHITECT Custom Log Homes • BUILDERS Steve Peckinpaugh and Custom Log Homes

Log builder Steve Peckinpaugh built this house for his parents in the Bitterroot Valley of Montana. Based in Stevensville, Montana, his log-building company has constructed hundreds of log houses over the last ten years.

Custom Log Homes prebuilds log houses at the company yard, then re-erects them on-site in locations from Alaska to Texas. The company offers in-house design services and will also build from owner-supplied plans.

Several interesting facets are apparent in this design. Breaking the long axis of the building with an angle renders it more compact and intriguing. Though not uncommon in conventional building, such a design is seldom seen in log structures because it requires more complicated notchwork.

The truncated roof is also different. In most designs, a return of such a short section of roof would be omitted, leaving instead a clean wall to the ridge. Returning the ridge keeps the building from looking too contemporary.

Concrete roofing tiles create a cover that will last as long as the rest of the building. But its heaviness requires that the structure be designed to support the weight. Here, Peckinpaugh has strengthened the overhang by using a knee brace under the eave log on the upper roof.

Today formal dining and living areas are more commonly combined than in the past, usually as a way of saving space.

A bedroom fireplace can be a cozy extra; however, most are seldom used and may be rather extravagant additions.

DOUBLE FORK RANCH

LOCATION Bitterroot Valley, Montana • ARCHITECT David Lorimer • BUILDER Mountain Log Homes

This striking home is located in central Montana on 6,000 acres of ranch land. Architect David Lorimer followed Frank Lloyd Wright's philosophy of designing for the site with little regard for local building traditions. Here, logs are combined with exposed concrete columns, steel, glass, and prodigious amounts of copper to create a high-tech look.

The house defies the normal parameters of log design. And while it may offend some, a more diverse audience will find it appealing. Says the owner, "I wanted logs in the house, but not a log house."

A noteworthy detail is a trussed girder on one side of the roof, along with an attendant chain hoist that is used to move large blocks of marble into the sculpture studio located above the carport.

Cut from nearby mountains, the logs used for the house

had been dead for many years. Their low moisture content minimized shrinkage. Log contraction and expansion is a problem when placing large amounts of glass in log walls. Here, in addition to using dry logs to prevent log movement, the architect also designed compression posts to strengthen the wall at points that lack interlocking logs. The posts run inside the logs and tie the plate log to the sill log, holding the wall in compression.

(A floor plan of this house is presented at the end of the book.)

Here in the bathroom, the glass bay doubles as an exit to the outdoors. Notice how the glass walls project from the logs.

The home's unconventional design for a log structure is reflected in almost every detail, including this contemporary stairway.

Inside the home, log walls are kept to a minimum, reflecting the owner's aesthetic preferences. This radical departure from tradition encompasses great expanses of glass, cement columns, and track lighting.

EAGLE CREEK VICTORIAN

LOCATION Eagle Creek, Idaho • ARCHITECT A. Lui Horstmeyer • BUILDERS Mountain Log Homes and owner

This pleasant mountain cottage has a storybook appeal. Its owners describe it as "a little bit Victorian," but its vintage is all its own.

The enchanting design is the result of blending different building styles and materials. The architect, of Sun Valley, Idaho, disdains log boxes. His solution in this case is a tri-level format incorporating traditional features like dormers, bays, and a cupola.

The dark-stained logs contrast pleasantly with pinstriped chinking and smooth stucco walls. The trim evokes the flavor of Tudor half-timbered construction.

When the owners took up residence on Christmas Day, there was no running water or electricity. They relied on the crackling warmth of a wood fire to keep winter at bay. Today, they continue to favor wood heat, using baseboard electricity for a backup.

By adding energy-saving features like an airlock entry and ventilated roof, the architect, builders, and owners have produced a practical yet beautiful home.

(A floor plan of this house is presented at the end of the book.)

Eagle Creek's two dormers with their half-moon windows are handsome, inside and out. They provide cozy, sunlit niches for desks or work tables.

The downstairs consists of a large kitchen and living room divided by a central stairway. On frosty mornings, woodstoves heat both rooms, and at meal time, the kitchen woodburner both provides room heat and cooks meals. On warmer days, a traditional oven can be used instead.

Furnished with grandmother's antiques, the living room is homey and inviting. Even the coffered ceiling has an old-fashioned feel, while the white ceiling squares lighten up the room.

Another quiet, window-lit corner of the house is just the place for this antique roll desk and dated rocking chair. Pictured on the wall is Idaho's famous Sun Valley ski area in its early days.

CONTEMPORARY LOG HOMES   147

EL RANCHO DELUXE

LOCATION North Fork, Idaho • BUILDER Hollis Poe

Log structures are distinctly compatible with a farm or ranch setting. Tradition plays an important role, but the organic nature of the buildings fits well in such surroundings. Whatever the reason, this small homestead north of Ketchum, Idaho, boasts ample rural charm.

The construction is simple, with a roof consisting of two intersecting gables. The pleasant design creates two covered porches by extending the roof eaves. Considering the amount of gear these owners have, the porches are a valuable asset.

With the first dusting of winter, feed is laid in for the horses and firewood is gathered for the long months ahead. The house is heated totally with wood, so the latter chore is not taken lightly.

An accessory task is checking between logs for cracks, then sealing them against cold winter winds—a minor but necessary duty associated with log-home living.

The assorted contents of this porch suggest a life-style compatible with its high-country Idaho environment.

CODY RUN

LOCATION Ketchum, Idaho • ARCHITECTS (DESIGNERS) Tom and Charlie Pomeroy •
BUILDERS Custom Log Homes and Pomeroy Brothers Construction

This second-story bay window provides additional space while brightening the dining room inside.

Here's a home designed to meet the needs and pleasures of its hardy owners and builders. A log ladder takes you straight up to the loft—quite a climb for a woman in heels!

A proper setting speaks highly for the home it hosts. Although this contemporary log house rests on a typical building lot in a small-town neighborhood, it fits its environment well: testimony to the fact that a "back forty" is not necessary to accommodate a log home.

The house features a two-story window wall to catch early light and a wraparound deck for following the sun throughout the day. It also boasts solar panels and radiant-slab heating.

This book emphasizes the special problems faced by homebuilders and homeowners in snow country, especially because many log houses are constructed in this environment. Strange accidents can occur during fierce winters, as the following incident illustrates.

After many winter storms, deep snow covered this home's roof. The sound construction of the house alleviated fear of structural failure. But as winter turned to spring, warming temperatures condensed the snow to ice several feet thick. One day, the ice slid from the upper roof and crashed onto the lower roof. Several hundred pounds broke through the skylight and landed on the bed below. Fortunately, no one was napping at the time.

(A floor plan of this house is presented at the end of the book.)

WARM SPRINGS

LOCATION Ketchum, Idaho • ARCHITECT Alpine Log Homes • BUILDERS Boender Construction and Alpine Log Homes

This quaint house is an example of a log structure's visual integration in a subdivision filled with conventional housing. Its overall form is Early American—but the painted trim and flower boxes create the charm of a European cottage.

The house is not large, compared to many of the other homes in this book. Living space is less than 2,000 square feet, giving the rooms an intimate yet functional appeal.

The use of logs as exposed floor joists is a strong rustic element. This effect is nicely balanced by the use of bright prints in the interior decor.

With living space under 2,000 square feet, this is not a large house, but little space is wasted. The rooms are both intimate and functionally appealing.

The home is located in an area of the Wood River Valley that is well known for its hot springs, which have been used for more than 100 years. Today, however, skiing is what brings most travelers to these parts. Nestled at the base of the surrounding hills, the house has a commanding view of Mount Baldy, one of the top ski mountains in the country.

(A floor plan of this house is presented at the end of the book.)

Logs serve as a strong visual element where used as exposed floor joists. In the living room, however, the owners chose to soften the effect with brightly patterned window curtains and papered walls.

ALDEN HOLLOW

LOCATION Wood River Valley, Idaho • ARCHITECT Steve Cook • BUILDER Dave Carter

As you might guess from its low profile, this home is earth-sheltered. Incorporating logs in such a home may be surprising, but the design developed by Steve Cook works exceedingly well. By keeping building elevations low and carefully berming around the house, the architect has accomplished two important goals—energy conservation and seclusion in an otherwise open environment.

Winter temperatures and winds in this part of the country can produce wind-chill factors of −60°F. Protecting the home from such extreme conditions is necessary if heat losses through walls and windows are to be kept under control. The earth berms accomplish this purpose: Only the roof is exposed to the chilly north.

An added benefit of the low-profile design is the privacy the berms provide. Despite being built near a major thoroughfare and adjacent housing, the home feels comfortably secluded.

(A floor plan of this house is presented at the end of the book.)

There's no shortage of wood finish in the kitchen. Pine floors, a massive wood slab countertop, and the 150-year-old unpeeled pine post bring the outdoors in.

This solarium was a late addition to the house. Warmed in winter by the nearly constant rays of Idaho's Sun Valley sun, the room adds considerably to the energy efficiency of the home.

GOOSE HOLLOW FARM

LOCATION Boulder County, Colorado • ARCHITECT Owner • BUILDERS Bob Reasor and Mark Younghein

In what can best be described as traditional ranch house architecture, this home on the front range of the Colorado Rockies has an interior design influenced by Early American, Victorian, and contemporary Western motifs.

Surrounding the massive stone chimney and fireplace is an interesting mixture of marble floors, wild-game mounts, and custom cabinetry incorporated into the rock work. The chimney serves as the principal divider of the down-stairs living space with the kitchen and dining rooms on one side and the sunken living room on the other. Since the kitchen is open to the dining room, the solarium, and several entrances, family members working in the kitchen do not feel isolated from the rest of the house.

While interior design and decorating are important to any home, it is interesting to see how flexible one can be with a log home. The rustic ambience so often associated with log homes is just one of many possibilities. Ultimately the choice of interior design is not predicated on the logs but on the owner's wishes.

The lamp post reflects this home's ranch-style motif, while covered, wrap-around porches are virtually mandatory in traditional western designs.

Note the double-chord truss overhead. The log members carry much of the roof weight, resulting in an interior uncluttered by posts. Interesting, too, is the massive chimney with built-in cabinets and corner fireplace. The living room's fireplace is on the opposite side of the chimney.

The living room is accented by its polished marble stairs and hearth. The decor is a mixture of cowboy comfort and refined elegance, reflecting the varied tastes of its owners. Note the combination of rock and wood, glass and leather.

FLOOR PLANS

On the following pages, we present the floor plans of selected homes shown earlier in the book.

MARIAH

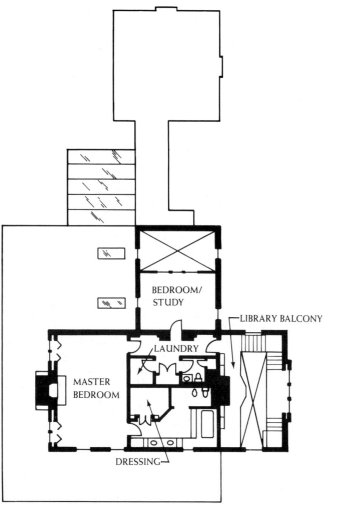

SECOND FLOOR

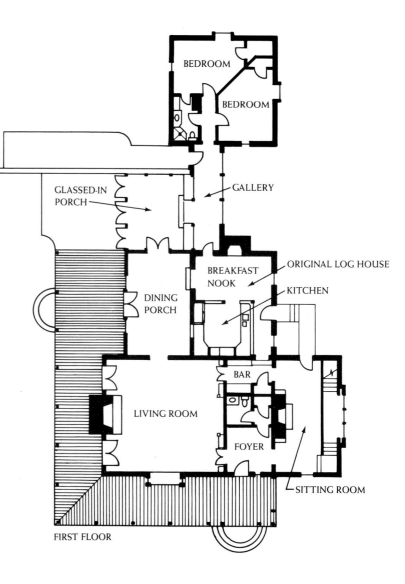

FIRST FLOOR

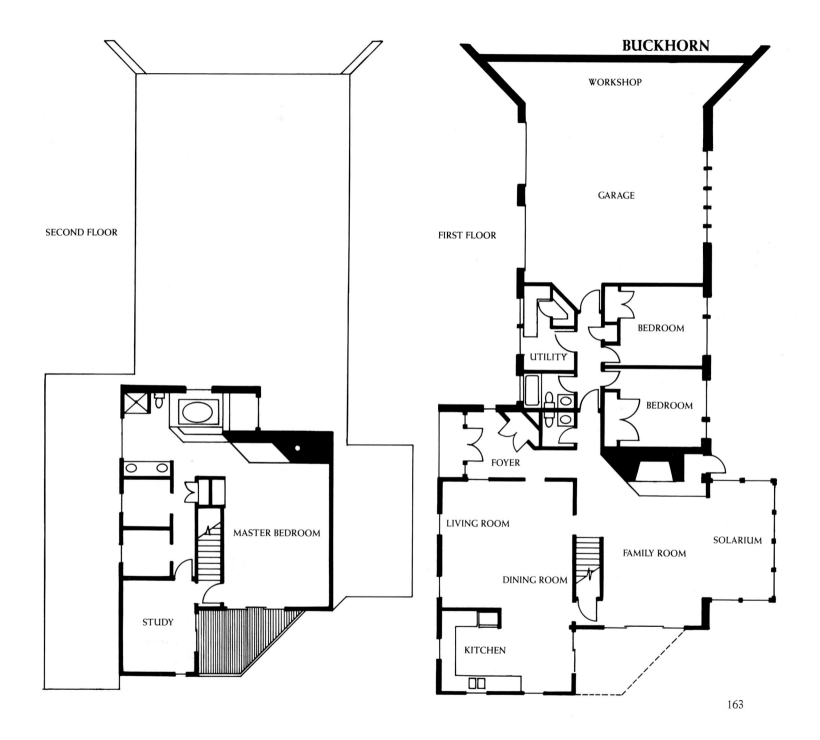

BUCKHORN

WORKSHOP

GARAGE

FIRST FLOOR

BEDROOM

UTILITY

BEDROOM

FOYER

LIVING ROOM

SOLARIUM

FAMILY ROOM

DINING ROOM

KITCHEN

SECOND FLOOR

MASTER BEDROOM

STUDY

163

CULLODEN FARM

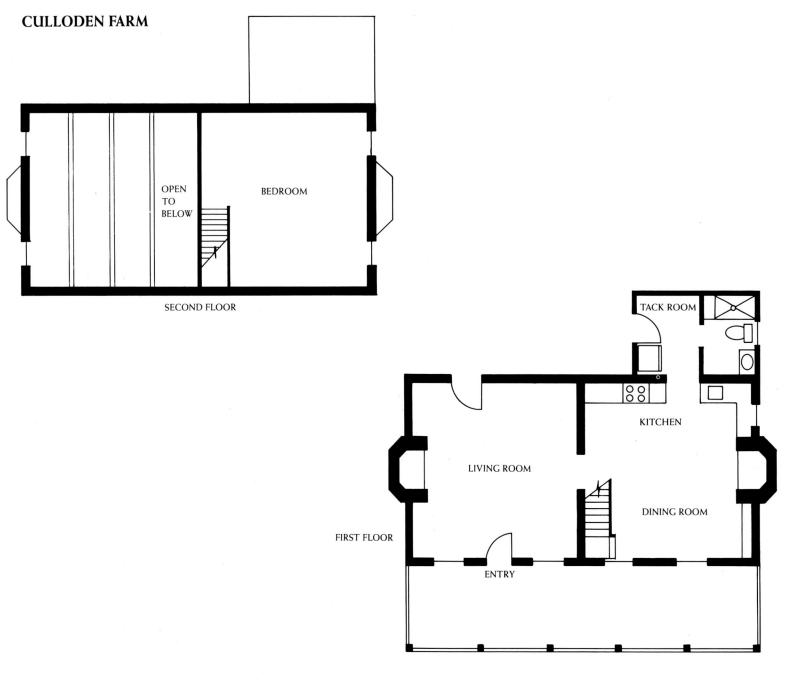

OPEN
TO
BELOW

BEDROOM

SECOND FLOOR

TACK ROOM

KITCHEN

LIVING ROOM

DINING ROOM

FIRST FLOOR

ENTRY

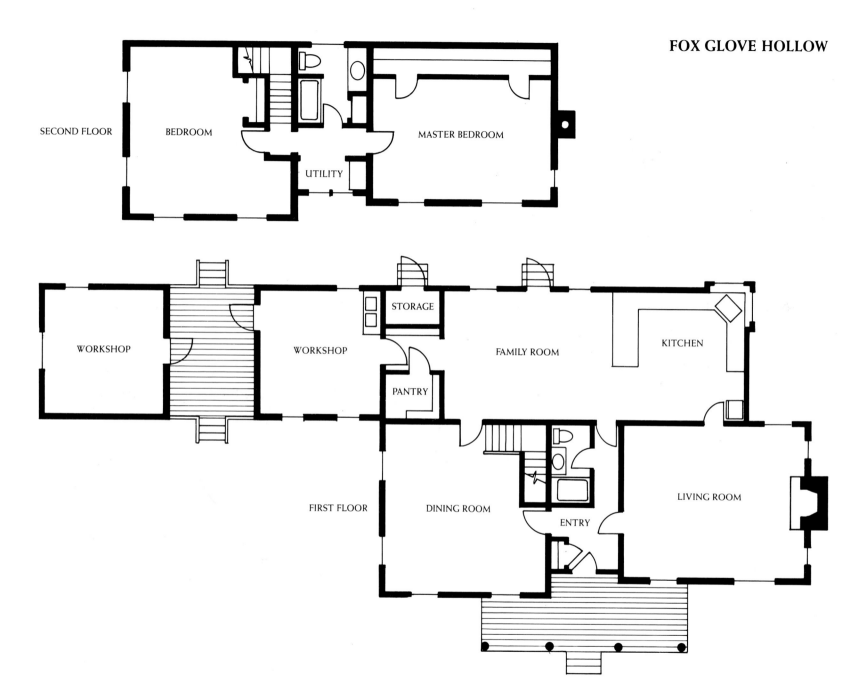

FOX GLOVE HOLLOW

SECOND FLOOR

BEDROOM

MASTER BEDROOM

UTILITY

WORKSHOP

WORKSHOP

STORAGE

FAMILY ROOM

KITCHEN

PANTRY

FIRST FLOOR

DINING ROOM

ENTRY

LIVING ROOM

165

LAKE HOUSE

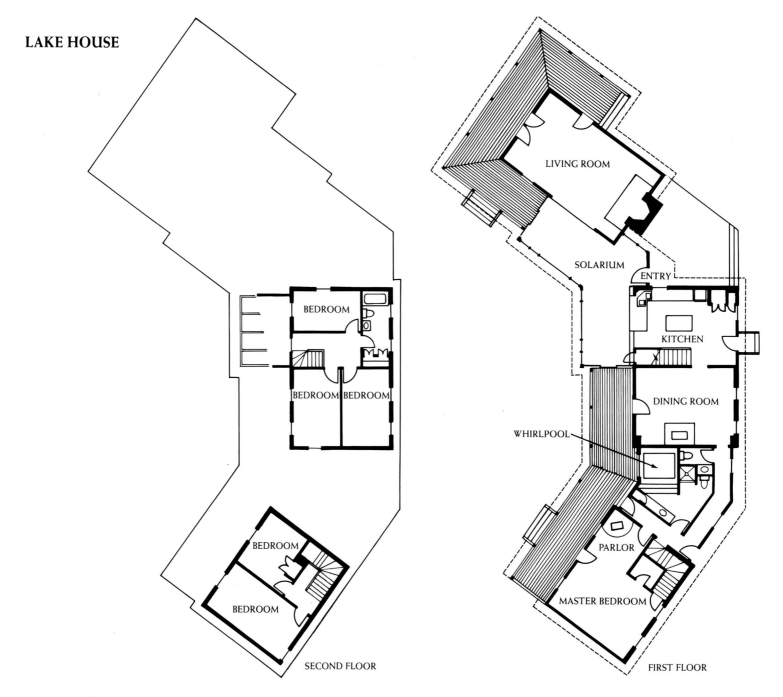

BEDROOM

BEDROOM BEDROOM

BEDROOM

BEDROOM

SECOND FLOOR

LIVING ROOM

SOLARIUM

ENTRY

KITCHEN

DINING ROOM

WHIRLPOOL

PARLOR

MASTER BEDROOM

FIRST FLOOR

166

PANTHER PLACE

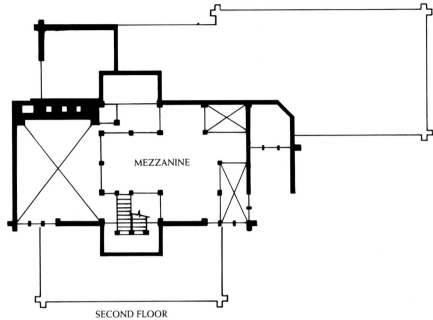

MEZZANINE

SECOND FLOOR

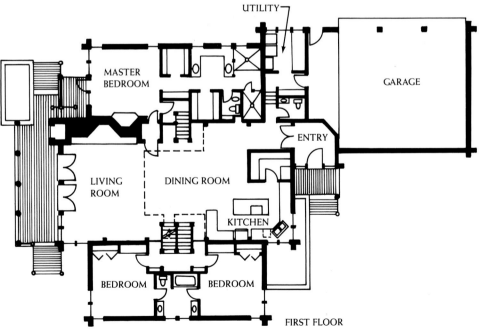

UTILITY

MASTER
BEDROOM

GARAGE

ENTRY

LIVING
ROOM

DINING ROOM

KITCHEN

BEDROOM

BEDROOM

FIRST FLOOR

167

ARROW RANCH

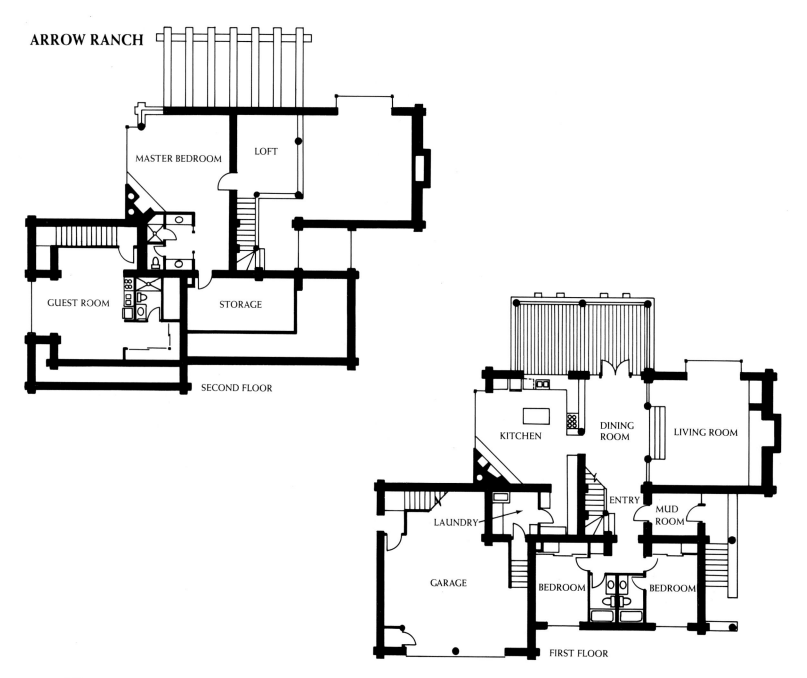

MASTER BEDROOM

LOFT

GUEST ROOM

STORAGE

SECOND FLOOR

KITCHEN

DINING ROOM

LIVING ROOM

LAUNDRY

ENTRY

MUD ROOM

GARAGE

BEDROOM

BEDROOM

FIRST FLOOR

168

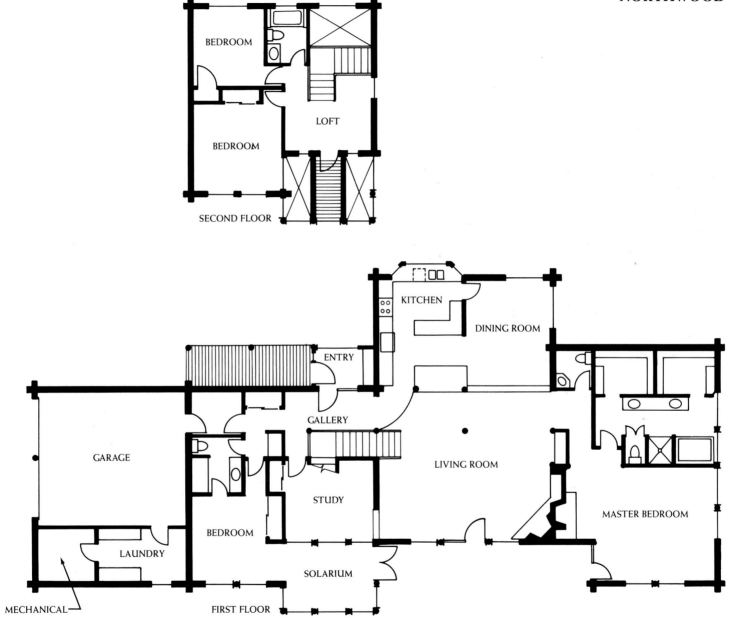

NORTHWOOD

BEDROOM

BEDROOM

LOFT

SECOND FLOOR

KITCHEN

DINING ROOM

ENTRY

GALLERY

GARAGE

LIVING ROOM

STUDY

BEDROOM

MASTER BEDROOM

LAUNDRY

SOLARIUM

MECHANICAL

FIRST FLOOR

169

BEAVER SPRINGS

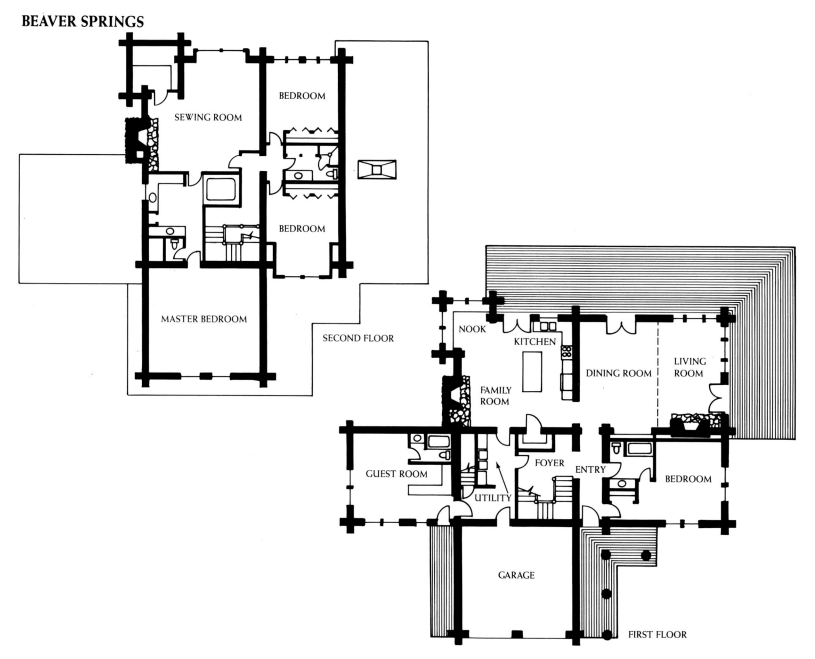

SEWING ROOM

BEDROOM

BEDROOM

MASTER BEDROOM

SECOND FLOOR

NOOK

KITCHEN

DINING ROOM

LIVING ROOM

FAMILY ROOM

GUEST ROOM

FOYER

ENTRY

BEDROOM

UTILITY

GARAGE

FIRST FLOOR

170

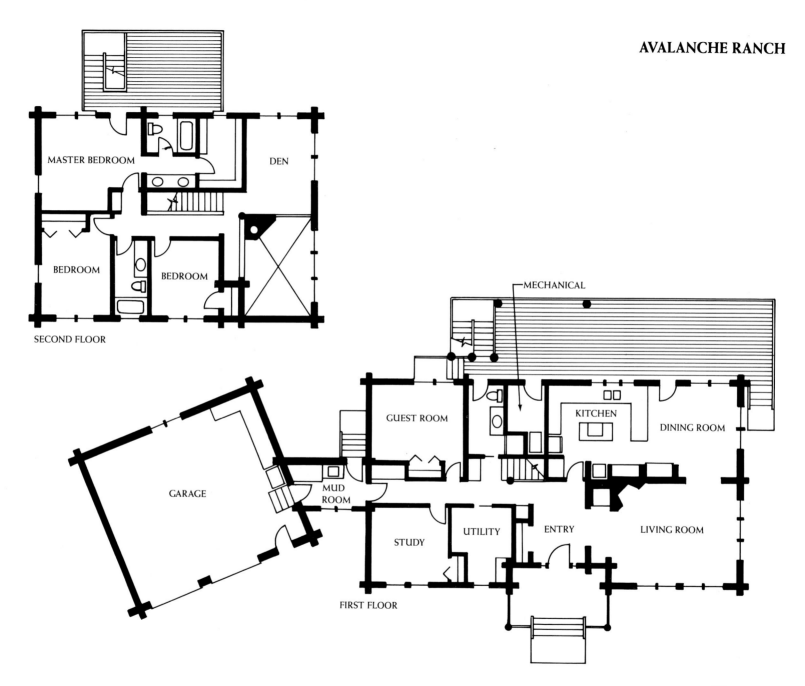

AVALANCHE RANCH

MASTER BEDROOM

DEN

BEDROOM

BEDROOM

SECOND FLOOR

MECHANICAL

GUEST ROOM

KITCHEN

DINING ROOM

GARAGE

MUD
ROOM

STUDY

UTILITY

ENTRY

LIVING ROOM

FIRST FLOOR

171

LEADVILLE

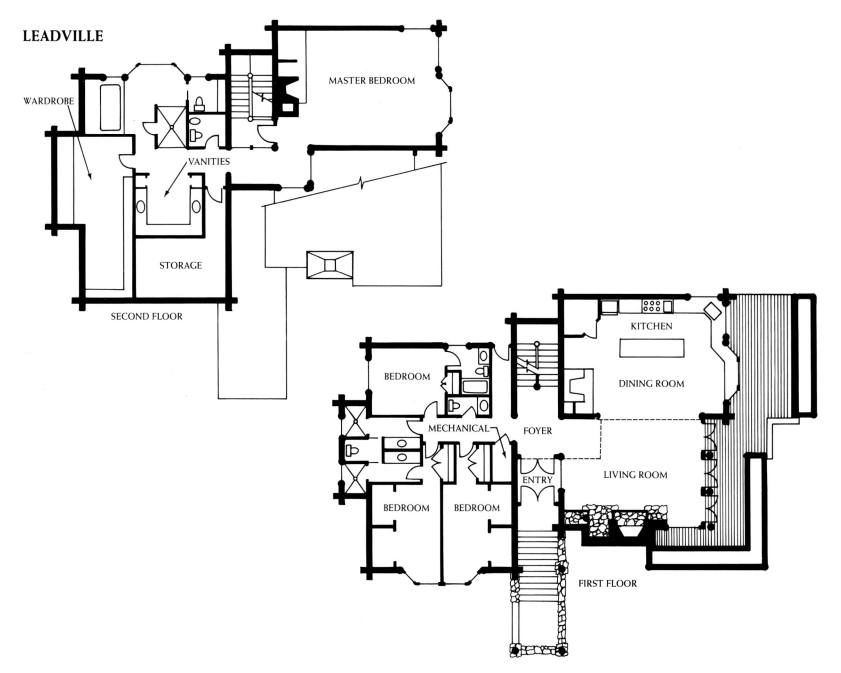

WARDROBE

VANITIES

MASTER BEDROOM

STORAGE

SECOND FLOOR

KITCHEN

BEDROOM

MECHANICAL

FOYER

DINING ROOM

BEDROOM

BEDROOM

ENTRY

LIVING ROOM

FIRST FLOOR

172

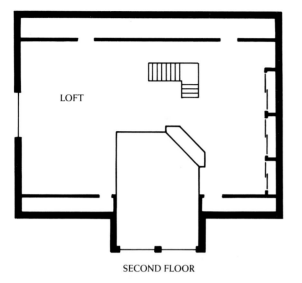

SECOND FLOOR

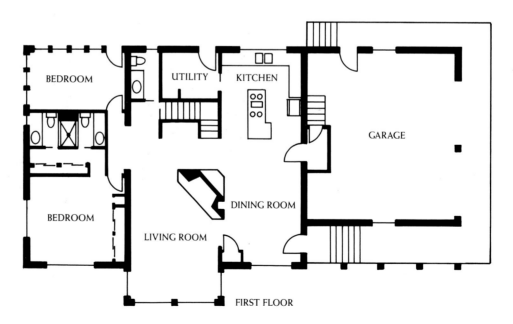

FIRST FLOOR

SUMMIT HOUSE

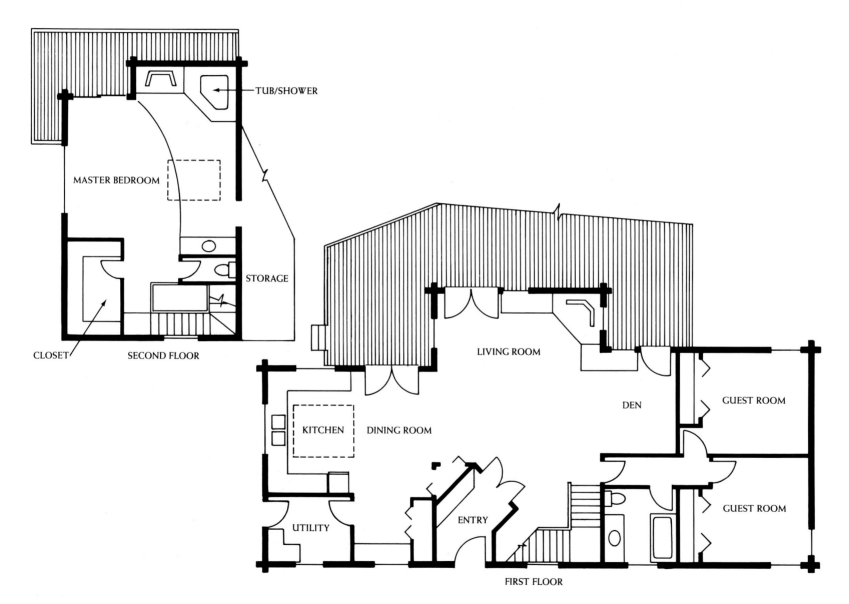

TUB/SHOWER

MASTER BEDROOM

STORAGE

CLOSET

SECOND FLOOR

LIVING ROOM

DEN

GUEST ROOM

KITCHEN

DINING ROOM

GUEST ROOM

UTILITY

ENTRY

FIRST FLOOR

174

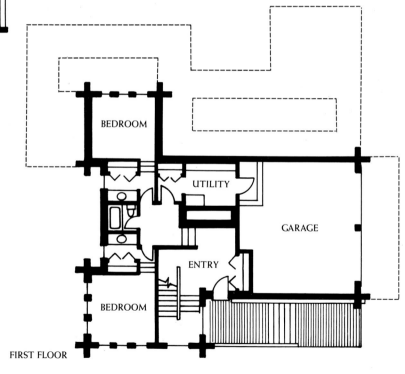

DINING
ROOM

HOT
TUB

LIVING ROOM

KITCHEN

MASTER
BEDROOM

SECOND FLOOR

BEDROOM

UTILITY

GARAGE

ENTRY

BEDROOM

FIRST FLOOR

175

RUSHING WATERS

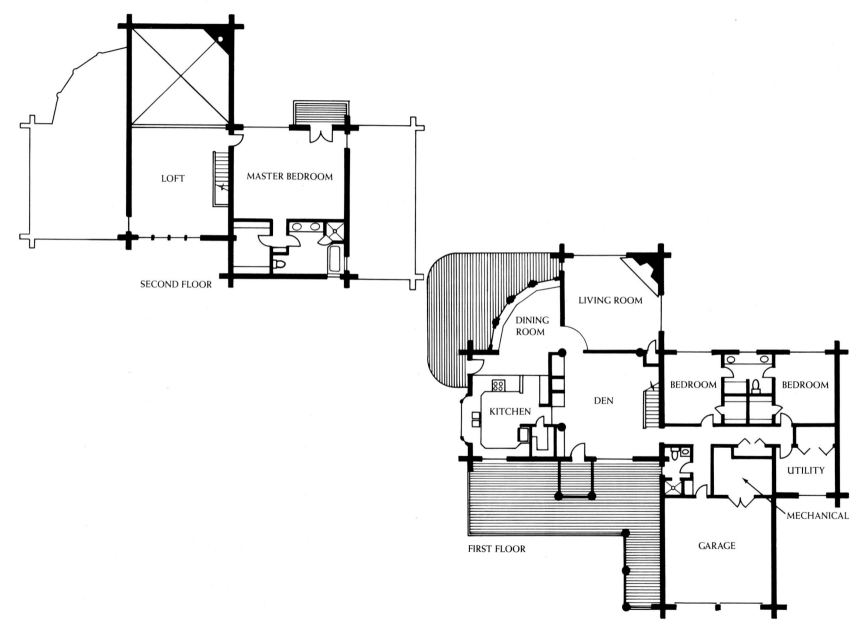

LOFT

MASTER BEDROOM

SECOND FLOOR

LIVING ROOM

DINING ROOM

BEDROOM

BEDROOM

DEN

KITCHEN

UTILITY

MECHANICAL

FIRST FLOOR

GARAGE

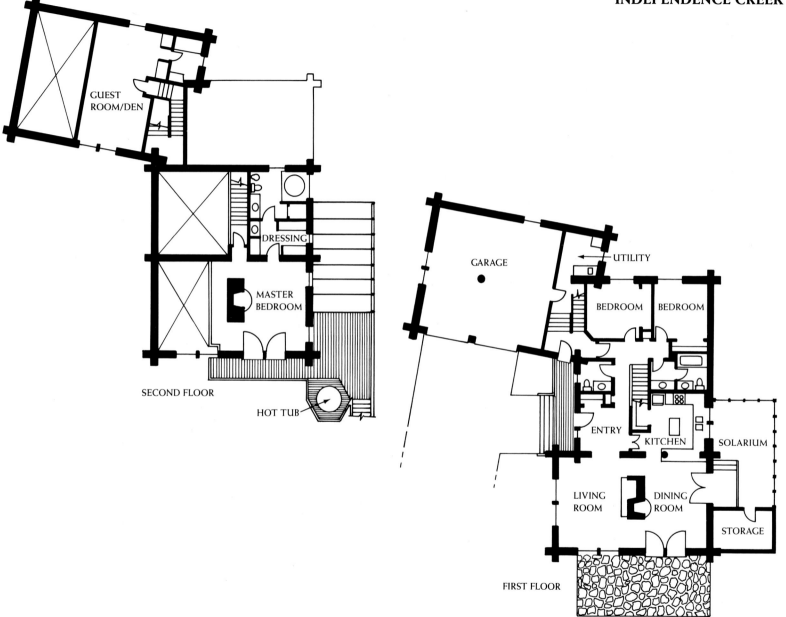

INDEPENDENCE CREEK

GUEST ROOM/DEN

DRESSING

MASTER BEDROOM

SECOND FLOOR

HOT TUB

GARAGE

UTILITY

BEDROOM   BEDROOM

ENTRY

KITCHEN

SOLARIUM

LIVING ROOM

DINING ROOM

STORAGE

FIRST FLOOR

177

WILD TURKEY RIDGE

LIVING ROOM

DINING ROOM

STUDY

KITCHEN

SECOND FLOOR

BEDROOM

THIRD FLOOR

BEDROOM

KITCHEN

LAUNDRY

BEDROOM

BASEMENT APARTMENT

BEDROOM

FIRST FLOOR

178

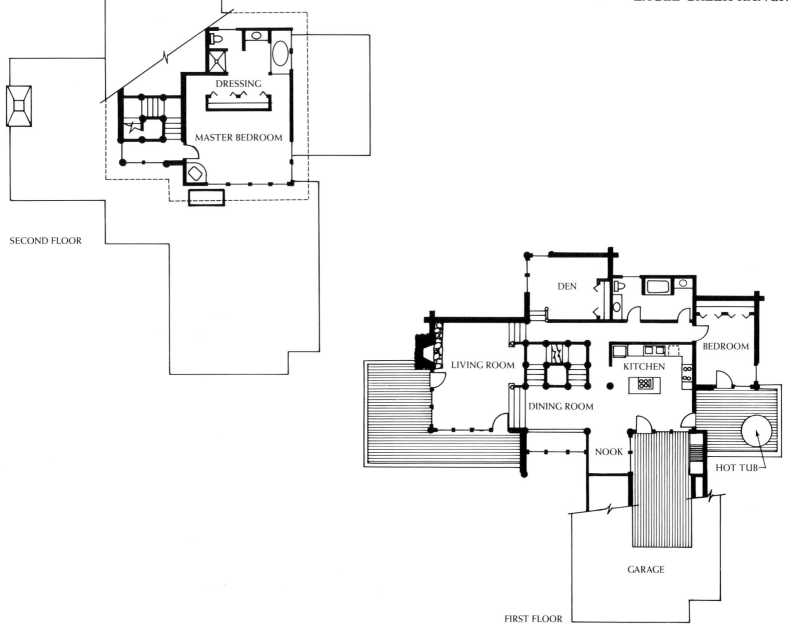

EAGLE CREEK RANCH

DRESSING

MASTER BEDROOM

SECOND FLOOR

DEN

BEDROOM

LIVING ROOM

KITCHEN

DINING ROOM

NOOK

HOT TUB

GARAGE

FIRST FLOOR

179

WHISPERING PINES

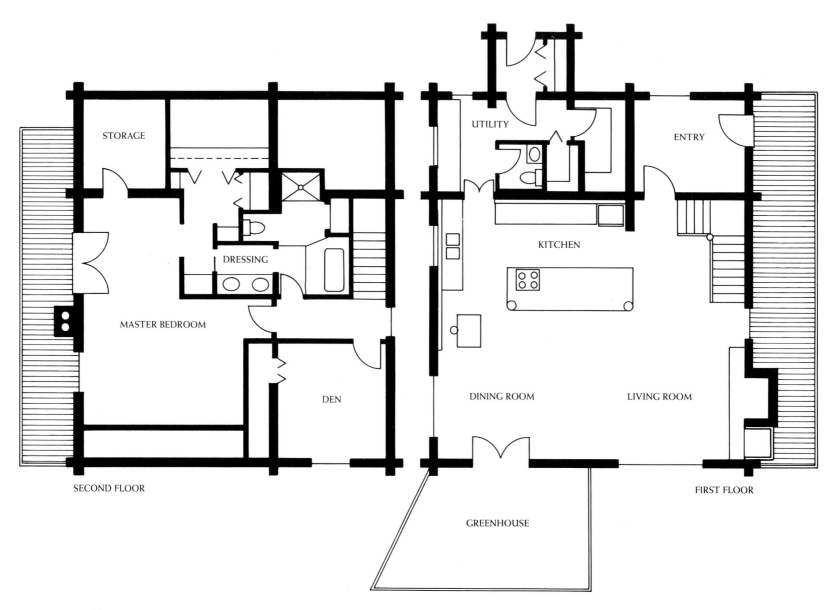

STORAGE

UTILITY

ENTRY

DRESSING

KITCHEN

MASTER BEDROOM

DEN

DINING ROOM

LIVING ROOM

SECOND FLOOR

FIRST FLOOR

GREENHOUSE

DOUBLE FORK RANCH

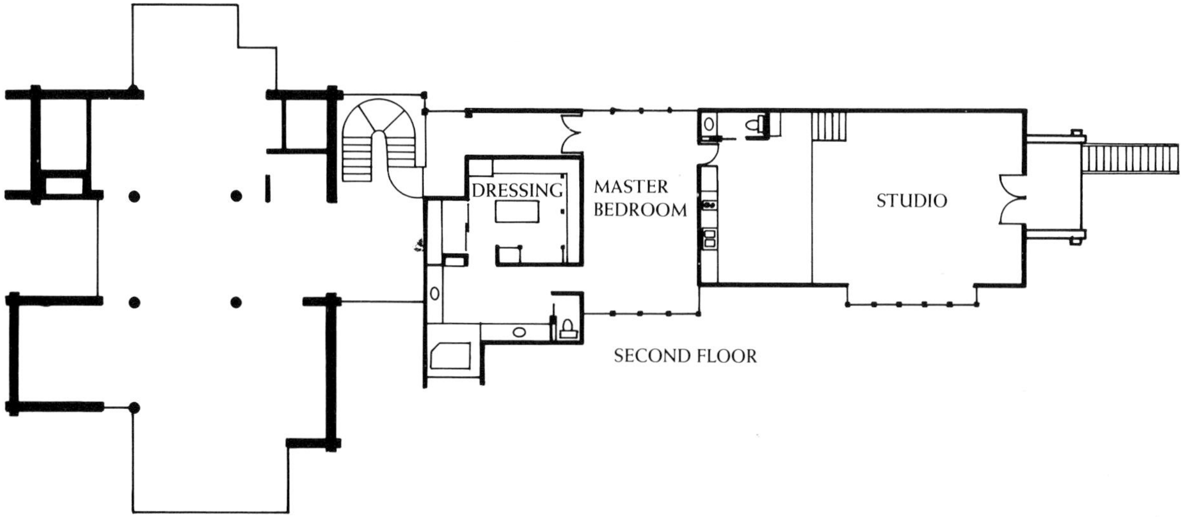

DRESSING

MASTER
BEDROOM

STUDIO

SECOND FLOOR

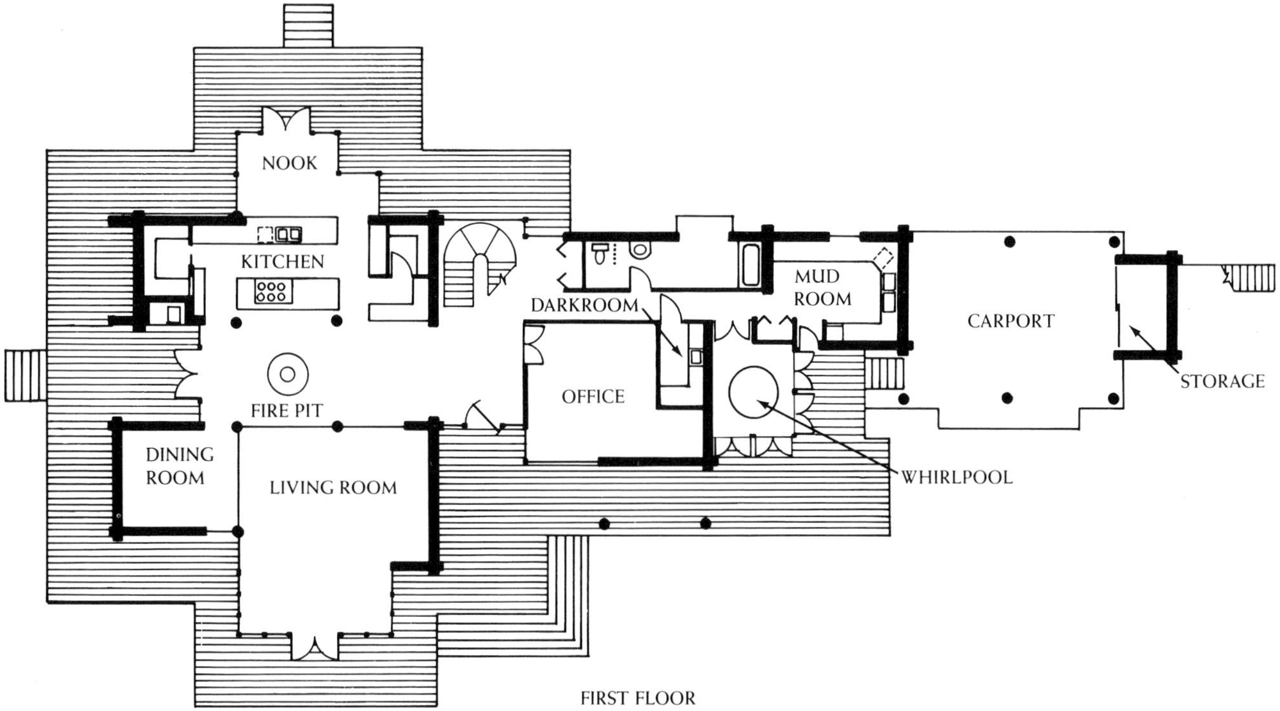

NOOK

KITCHEN

DARKROOM

MUD
ROOM

CARPORT

STORAGE

FIRE PIT

OFFICE

WHIRLPOOL

DINING
ROOM

LIVING ROOM

FIRST FLOOR

EAGLE CREEK VICTORIAN

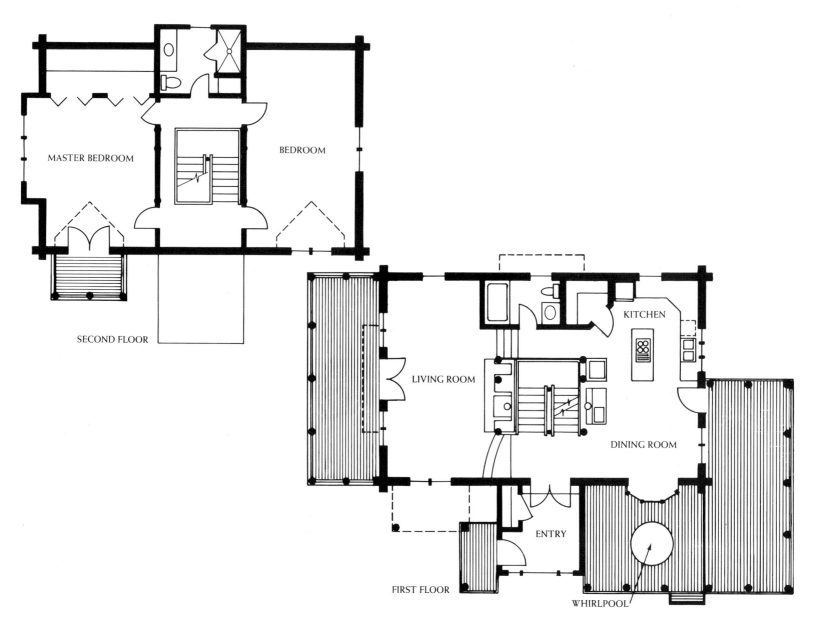

MASTER BEDROOM

BEDROOM

SECOND FLOOR

LIVING ROOM

KITCHEN

DINING ROOM

ENTRY

FIRST FLOOR

WHIRLPOOL

182

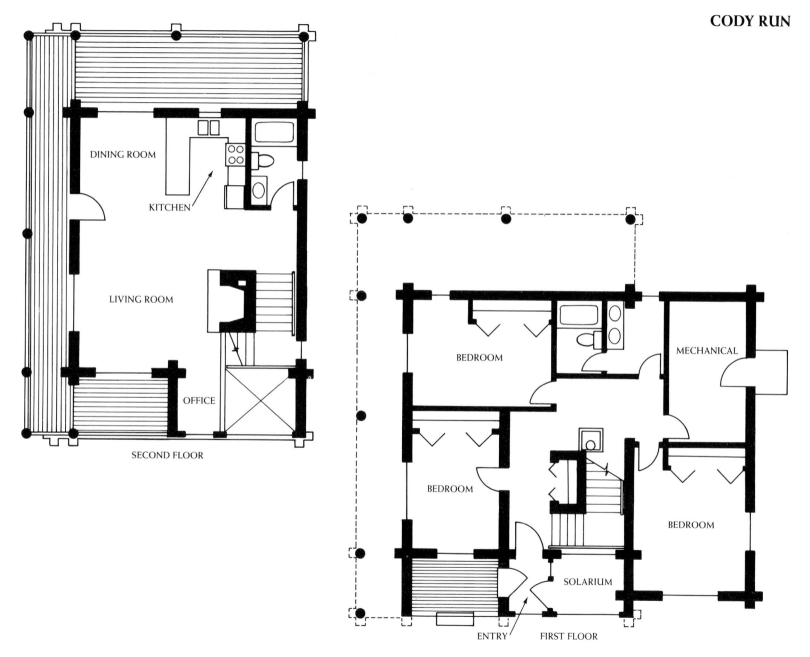

CODY RUN

DINING ROOM

KITCHEN

LIVING ROOM

OFFICE

SECOND FLOOR

BEDROOM

MECHANICAL

BEDROOM

BEDROOM

SOLARIUM

ENTRY

FIRST FLOOR

183

WARM SPRINGS

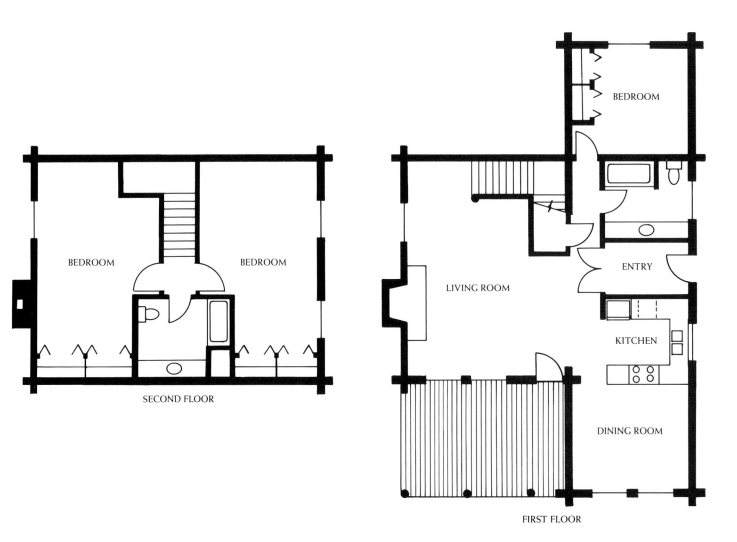

BEDROOM

BEDROOM

BEDROOM

SECOND FLOOR

LIVING ROOM

ENTRY

KITCHEN

DINING ROOM

FIRST FLOOR

184

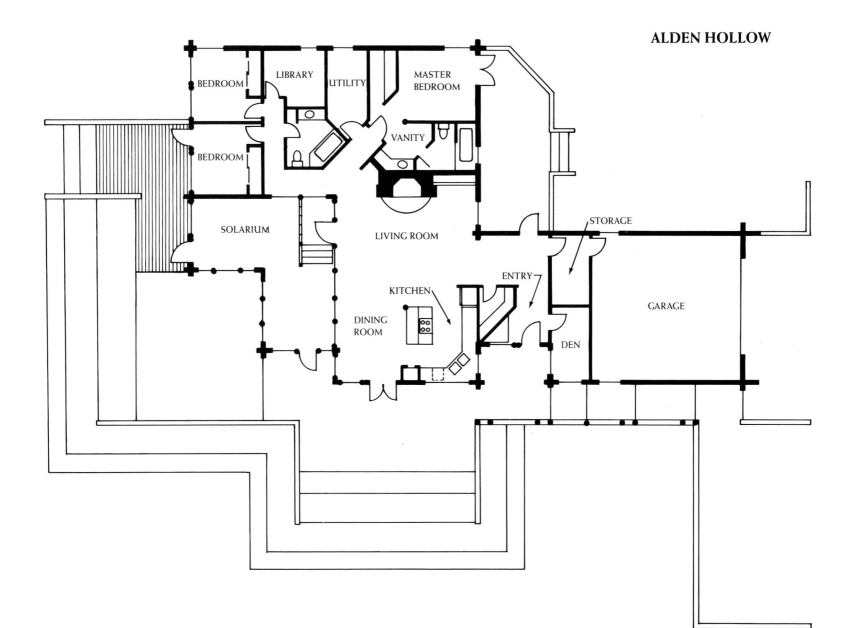

ALDEN HOLLOW

BEDROOM

LIBRARY

UTILITY

MASTER
BEDROOM

BEDROOM

VANITY

SOLARIUM

LIVING ROOM

STORAGE

ENTRY

GARAGE

KITCHEN

DINING
ROOM

DEN

ARCHITECTS AND DESIGNERS OF LOG HOMES

It is impossible to list all the fine architects and designers who are creating log homes today. Still, we want to present at least a partial list, as an aid to you should you want to build a log home. The professionals listed here are people we have met; in most cases, we have seen examples of their work, some of which is included in this book. While we feel that all of these individuals are competent in the field of log-home design, we don't endorse or represent them to be the most qualified in their field. You may find equally qualified designers in your area. To seek the names of local designers, you can contact the organizations listed at the end of this appendix.

LISTING

Architectural Associates of Crested Butte
617 Maroon, Third Floor
P.O. Box 1209
Crested Butte, CO 81224

David Barovetto
P.O. Box 269
Sun Valley, ID 83353

Dale Bates
P.O. Box 2012
Ketchum, ID 83340

Steve Cook
P.O. Box 680
Ketchum, ID 83340

John Daley
P.O. Box 1507
Sun Valley, ID 83353

Jay Dalgliesh
P.O. Box 2555
Charlottesville, VA 22902

Arthur A. Hannafin
1007 North Nevada Street
Carson City, NV 89701

A. Lui Horstmeyer
P.O. Box 1205
Sun Valley, ID 83353

Janet Jarvis
P.O. Box 1183
Ketchum, ID 83340

David Lorimer
1747 Hancock Street
San Diego, CA 92101

McLaughlin Architects Chartered
P.O. Box 479
Sun Valley, ID 83353

Darryl McMillen
209 Broadway
P.O. Box 1068
Sun Valley, ID 83353

Stephen V. Miller
P.O. Box 566
Nashville, IN 47448

Jack Murchie
18 South Michigan Avenue
Chicago, IL 60603

Jim Ruscitto, Nicholas Latham, and Thadd Blanton
Ruscitto, Latham and Blanton
P.O. Box 419
Sun Valley, ID 83353

Ralph Rutter
P.O. Box 3059
Ketchum, ID 83340

David A. Schlechten
P.O. Box 1027
Hamilton, MT 59840

Helen Ziegler
P.O. Box 2020
Ketchum, ID 83340

ORGANIZATIONS

Home Manufacturers Council
15th and M Streets NW
Washington, DC 20005

Canadian Log Builders Association
P.O. Box 403
Prince George, British Columbia
Canada V2L 4S2

BUILDERS OF LOG HOMES

As with the list of architects presented in the previous section, the following list of professional log-home builders represents only a small segment of the total number of practicing log builders. Many of the individuals listed here are represented by homes shown earlier in this book. Each builder in the list is an individual whose work we have seen and judged highly competent.

To seek the names of other log builders in your area, contact the organizations listed at the end of the previous section.

LISTING

David Ash
P.O. Box 556
Seeley Lake, MT 59868

John Beauregard
P.O. Box 770974
Steamboat Springs, CO 80477

Tom Blanchard
P.O. Box 225
Bellevue, ID 83313

Matthew Brothers Construction
Swan Valley Route
Box 2301
Seeley Lake, MT 59868

W. Crosby Brown
R.R. 1, Box 229
Washington, MO 63090

Jim Budge
P.O. Box 1497
Jackson, WY 83001

Steve Cappellucci
P.O. Box 429
Almont, CO 81210

Rob Carrick
P.O. Box 104
Woody Creek, CO 81656

Dave Carter
Box 23
Ketchum, ID 83340

Rex Christiansen
Route 1, Box 3595
Driggs, ID 83422

John Daley
P.O. Box 1507
Sun Valley, ID 83353

Peter Dembergh
P.O. Box 1503
Ketchum, ID 83340

Rick DeSelm
Box 126
Dolores, CO 81323

Aaron Downey
1143 NE Willow Creek Road
Corvallis, MT 59828

Peter Gott
Route 3, Box 275
Marshall, NC 28753

Arthur A. Hannafin
1007 North Nevada Street
Carson City, NV 89701

Mike Hautzenroder
122 Essex South
Lexington Park, MD 20653

Krissa Johnson
Adirondack Log Building
Averyville Road
P.O. Box 347
Lake Placid, NY 12946

John Lloyd
P.O. Box 265
Ketchum, ID 83340

Jack Loughran
P.O. Box 223
Eagle, CO 81631

Charles McRaven
P.O. Box G
Free Union, VA 22940

Mike Nickels
R.R. 4, Box 172
Nashville, IN 47448

Gary Pendergrass
Elsie, Route 561
Seaside, OR 97138

Morton Riddle IV
Route 2, Box 853
Purcellville, VA 22132

Ralph Rutter
P.O. Box 3059
Ketchum, ID 83340

Don Shultz
Highway 321
Gatlinburg, TN 37738

Tim Starr
P.O. Box 3006
Truckee, CA 95734

Richard Stopol
Box 1281
Hailey, ID 83333

Ben Tate
8396 Sunnyside Road
Sandpoint, ID 83864

Art Thiede
P.O. Box 3308
Ketchum, ID 83340

Richard Tuxbury
P.O. Box 331
Traverse City, MI 49685

Les Weber
P.O. Box 396
Jackson, WY 83001

Mark Younghein
Colorado Custom Log Homes
P.O. Box 48
Lyons, CO 80540

LOG-HOME COMPANIES

While most of the homes pictured in *American Log Homes* were custom designed and built, many of the basic log shells were prebuilt by log-home companies. Though there are well over one hundred such companies throughout the United States and Canada, the following companies are mentioned because they either were involved in the homes featured in this book or because we are familiar with their product. For a complete listing of log-home companies, you should consult the two publications listed at the end of this appendix.

LISTING

Alpine Log Homes
P.O. Box 85
Victor, MT 59875

Custom Log Homes
Drawer 226
Stevensville, MT 59870

Heritage Log Homes
Box 610, Highway 321
Gatlinburg, TN 37738

Joseph Log Homes
P.O. Box 696
Joseph, OR 97846

Maple Island Log Homes
P.O. Box 331
Traverse City, MI 49684

Mountain Log Homes
P.O. Box 1128
Hamilton, MT 59840

Neville's Log Homes
West Fork Route
Darby, MT 59829

Rocky Mountain Log Homes
3353 Highway 93 South
Hamilton, MT 59840

The Timber Touch
P.O. Box 153
Nevada City, CA 95959

PUBLICATIONS

The Log Home Annual
Home Buyer Publications
P.O. Box 2078
Falls Church, VA 22042

Log Home Guide for Builders and Buyers
Muir Publishing Company
Exit 447, Interstate 40
Hartford, TN 37753

BIBLIOGRAPHY

Bealer, A., and J. O. Ellis. *The Log Cabin — Homes of the North American Wilderness*. Barre, Mass.: Barre Publishing, 1978.

Brumfield, William C. *Gold in Azure*. Boston: David R. Godine, Publisher, 1983.

Fiodorov, B., S. Vikulov, V. Savik, and N. Johnstone. *Architecture of the Russian North*. Leningrad: Aurora Art Publishers, 1976.

Foley, Mary Mix. *The American House*. New York: Harper and Row, 1980.

Franzwa, G. M. *The Story of Old Ste. Genevieve*. 2d ed. Gerald, Mo.: Patrice Press, 1973.

Kirschenbaum, H., S. Schafstall, and J. Stuchin. *The Adirondack Guide*. Raquette Lake, N.Y.: Sagamore Institute, 1983.

Langsner, D. *A Logbuilder's Handbook*. Emmaus, Pa.: Rodale Press, 1982.

Mackie, Allan B. *Building with Logs*. Prince George, British Columbia: Log Homes Publications, 1977.

McRaven, Charles. *Building the Hewn Log House*. New York: Harper and Row, 1978.

Mann, D., and R. Skinulis. *The Complete Log House Book*. New York: McGraw-Hill Ryerson, 1979.

Muir, Doris. *Log Home Guide*. Gardenvale, Quebec: Muir Publishing Co., various issues.

Pinkerton, Joan Trego. *Knights of the Broadax*. Caldwell, Idaho: The Caxton Printers, 1981.

Suzuki, M. *Wooden Houses*. Edited by Y. Futagawa. Introduction by C. Norberg-Schulz. New York: Harry N. Abrams, 1979.

INDEX

Page numbers in *italic* indicate floor plans.